L'Chayim

To Life

by

Sanford R. Howard

SAN® *Enterprises Inc*

P. O. Box 623

Thorsby, AL 35171-0623

Cover Credits:
Cover by Leah Berkowitz
Book Layout by Reesa Richman and Obadiah Markowitz

SAN® *Enterprises*
P. O. Box 623 • Thorsby, AL 35171

Printed in the U.S.A.

ISBN: 0-9621661-1-1

Contents

BOOK 1

TO LIFE
L'CHAYIM

iv

BOOK 1

TO LIFE—
L'CHAYIM

BY

SANFORD R. HOWARD

Thou wilt shew me the path of life: in thy presence is fulness of joy; at thy right hand there are pleasures for evermore.

Psalm 16:11

v

CHAPTER 1

CONCEPTS OF THE MESSIAH– BIBLICAL AND TALMUDIC

The subject of The Messiah has been cherished in the history of Israel. In the Talmud it is taught: "All the prophets prophesied only for the Messianic age." **SHABBATH** 63a, volume 1, p. 295, Babylonian Talmud, Soncino Press.

THE JEWISH ENCYCLOPEDIA states: "the idea of a personal Messiah runs throughout the Old Testament [Holy Scriptures]. It is the natural outcome of the prophetic future hope." volume 8, p. 506, column 1, article "**Messiah**."

THE UNIVERSAL JEWISH ENCYCLOPEDIA, volume 7, p. 501, column 1, article "**Messiah**" states: " The idea of a personal Messiah has become so deeply rooted in the consciousness of the people that it is taken for granted in the rabbinic literature."

In the Talmud, the Midrash Rabbah, and most of the Prayer Books, we find that ancient Israel's Messianic hope has been cherished by our Jewish people throughout the centuries, including the present. Many, it is true, have lost the knowledge that God gave us as a people. It is therefore fitting that we review at this time. Throughout the world untold numbers of the Jewish people often recite the "Thirteen Principles of the Faith" as stated by Maimonides in the 12th century C. E.. Article 12 states: "I believe with perfect faith in the coming of the Messiah, and though He tarry, I will wait daily for His coming." **DAILY PRAYER BOOK,** p.165, Hebrew Publishing Company.

One of the precious promises given to Israel is found in Isaiah 59:20. "A redeemer will come to Zion, and unto them that turn from transgression in Jacob, saith the Lord." In the Talmud, "R. Jonathan said: Great is repentance, because it brings about redemption, as it is said, <u>And a redeemer will come to Zion, and unto them that turn from transgression in Jacob</u> [Isaiah 59:20], i.e., why will a redeemer come to Zion? Because of those that turn from transgression in Jacob." **YOMA** 86b, p. 428.

Amos, who prophesied shortly before Isaiah, made this inspired prediction concerning Israel's future. "In that day I

will raise up the tabernacle of David that is fallen, and close up
the breaches thereof, and I will raise up his ruins, and I will
build it as in the days of old." Amos 9:11. The Talmud,
commenting on this Messianic prophecy, quotes Rabbi Isaac
concerning the Messiah, as given by Rabbi Nahman, "Even so,
he rejoiced, as it is written, <u>In that day I will raise up the
tabernacle of David</u> ha-nofeleth [that is fallen]. He replied,
Thus hath R. Johanan said: In the generation when the son of
David [i.e. Messiah] will come, scholars will be few in number,
and for the rest, their eyes will fail through sorrow and grief."
-**SANHEDRIN** 96b, 97a, volume 2, p. 654, Soncino Press.
The statement made by Rabbi Johanan that there will be few
real scholars at the time of the Messiah's coming is revealing.
Today, it can be said that the number of scholars who believe
and teach the Biblical prophecies and promises that The
Messiah, as son of king David and as heir to his throne, will
come, are few. However, that belief abounds in most of our
current Prayer Books as a legacy from our forefathers. Here is
a good example: "O God and God of our fathers! May our
remembrance rise and come and be accepted before Thee, with
the remembrance of our fathers, of Messiah the son of David
Thy servant, of Jerusalem Thy holy city, and of all Thy people
the house of Israel, bringing deliverance and well-being, grace,
lovingkindness and mercy, life and peace on this Day Of
Atonement." **Prayer Book for the Day of Atonement**, pp. 29,
30,127,179, Dr. A. Th. Phillips, Hebrew Publishing Company.
Also see **Daily Prayers** revised, pp. 201,227,255,293-
a,343,425,567,599-601,675, and **Day of Atonement**, section 1,
pp. 23,24, section 2, pp. 46,80, English edition, Dr. H. Adler,
Hebrew Book Company.
    The question arises; When will The Messiah, the son of
David, come to deliver God's faithful people?   The Holy
Scriptures in Daniel 12:1-4 states: "At that time shall Michael
stand up, the great Prince which standeth for the children of thy
people: and there shall be a time of trouble, such as never was
since there was a nation even to that same time: and at that time
thy people shall be delivered, every one that shall be found
written in the book. And many of them that sleep in the dust of
the earth shall awake, some to everlasting life, and some to
shame and everlasting contempt. And they that be wise shall
shine as the brightness of the firmament; and they that turn
many to righteousness as the stars forever and ever. But thou,
O Daniel, shut up the book, even to the time of the end: many

shall run to and fro, and knowledge shall be increased."
Commenting on Daniel 12, Dr. J.J. Slotki remarks: "This
chapter is generally taken by Jewish authorities to refer to the
remote future which will herald the advent of the Messianic
era." Additionally "to the time of the end" he says it means
"until the Messianic era." **Daniel, Ezra, Nehemiah,** pp. 100-
102.

The prophecy of Daniel said, "there shall be a time of
trouble, such as never was since there was a nation even to that
same time." We are already into that time, with the prospect of
still greater trouble ahead. Mankind is becoming more fearful
and desperate than ever as they contemplate future events.
Murders, wars, revolution, famine, earthquakes, floods, and
pestilence are constantly in the news. Trouble of every kind is
rampant, as was in the days of Noah when "the earth was
corrupt before God, and the earth was filled with violence."
Genesis 6:11. The horrific destructive weapons of the nuclear
age can make the "time of the end," "a time of trouble, such
as never was since there was a nation." This makes the
Messianic hope more relevant, for it assures us that, "at that
time thy people [God's faithful and true remnant people] shall
be delivered," and the righteous dead "who sleep in the dust of
the earth," shall be resurrected to everlasting life.

Note this significant prophecy in Hosea 3:4,5: "The
children of Israel shall abide many days without a king, and
without a prince, and without a sacrifice, and without an ephod,
and without teraphim. Afterward shall the children of Israel
return and seek the Lord their God and David their king; and
shall fear the Lord and His goodness in the later days."
Commenting on the prophecy in Hosea 3:4,5, Dr. A. Cohen
identifies the David in verse 5 as "The prototype of perfect
kingship (cf. Eze. xxxiv. 23). The Targum identifies him with
"the King Messiah."—**The Twelve Prophets,** p.13, Soncino
Press.

The Targum on Hosea 3:4,5 says, "The children of Israel
shall abide many days without a king of the house of David,
and without one who exerciseth dominion over Israel, or who
offereth sacrifices in Jerusalem and without ephod or
annunciation. Afterward shall the children of Israel return and
seek the service of the Lord their God, and be obedient to
Messiah, the son of David their king: and he shall teach them
the worship of the Lord, and increase the good that is to come
to them at the end of days." In the **Midrash Rabbah,** on

Genesis chapter 48, section 6, volume 1, p. 408, it says: "Thus, in the Messianic future Israel shall fear, viz. <u>And they shall come in fear unto the Lord and to His goodness</u> (Hos. iii,5)." Dr. Joseph Klausner states: " Not only did the name 'son of David' become a standing title of the King-Messiah, but also 'David' itself." He quotes Hosea 3:5 and certain Talmudic statements to support that usage. See his work **The Messianic Ideal in Israel,** p.21, Macmillian Company. On pages 46-48 he shows with accurate logic that the words "David their king" in that prophecy cannot literally mean that King David of ancient times will come to life to rule again over Israel, but Hosea refers to an individual personal Messiah, who, as "a strong redeemer," will reign over His people. Dr. A. Cohen, in his **Everyman's Talmud,** p. 347, E. P. Dutton & Company, ably shows that the David referred to in Hosea 3:4,5 is the King Messiah as the son of David and heir to his throne.

The divinely inspired prophecy of Hosea 3:4, 5 has been fulfilled with amazing accuracy. It is true that for "many days"— during the past 19 centuries since the destruction of Jerusalem and the Temple by the Roman armies in 70 C.E.— the children of Israel have been without a king, prince, sacrifice, image, ephod, and teraphim. Though deprived of so many precious privileges that our forefathers enjoyed in their own land, we have never lost hope, because we know that the God of Israel lives and loves those who are upright toward Him. The same prediction states that "<u>afterward</u> shall the children of Israel return, and seek the Lord and David their king; and shall fear the Lord and His goodness <u>in the latter days</u>." Yes! there is to be a turning of our sons and daughters to the God of our fathers "in the last days." And since king David has been dead for nearly 30 centuries, the "David their king" whom they shall seek can be none other than our Jewish Messiah the son of David. This has been our cherished hope throughout the centuries to the present time.

In the Yigdal which is recited as a summary of the Thirteen Principles of the Faith it says: "At the time of the end He [God] will send our Messiah to save all who wait for his final help."—**Daily Prayer Book,** p.14, Phillip Birnbaum, Hebrew Publishing Company. Also the **Prayer Book for the Day of Atonement,** pp. 62-a, 82; and **Daily Prayers,** pp. 17, 321, Dr. A. Th. Phillips, Hebrew Publishing Company. In Addition: **Day of Atonement,** section 1, p.76; section 2, p. 2, Dr. H. Adler, Star Hebrew Book Company.

In Deuteronomy 4:27, 30-32, the Lord gave Israel startling warning concerning the consequences of their failure to heed the instructions He gave in the Holy Scriptures: "The Lord shall scatter you among the peoples, and ye shall be left few in numbers among the nations, whither the Lord shall lead you away... In thy distress, when all these things are come upon thee, in the end of days, thou wilt return to the Lord your God, and hearken unto his voice; for the Lord thy God is a merciful God;... For ask now from one end of heaven unto the other, whether there hath been any such thing as this great thing is, or hath been heard like it?" Thus the Lord said that He would scatter Israel among the nations because of their disobedience. And He added "in the end of days"—literally [translated from] the Hebrew text "in the last days"—Jews would be few in number [a minority group] in the land of their dispersion. One of the worst periods of distress for our Jewish people was when Hitler engineered the extermination of the six million, from 1933-1945. Never before had an individual group of people been singled out for extermination because of their religion. This was a deliberately planned and executed genocide with tacit assent by almost the whole civilized world. What is this a sign of? It is a sign that we are living in the time of the end of this world and the soon coming of The Messiah. As we look at conditions in the world today, famine, flood, earthquake, and pestilence exist on a scale never known before. One can feel the expectation that something is about to occur. That occurrence, I submit, is God preparing to intervene and send The Messiah to deliver us from the hand of the destroyer [Satan].

Our Sages, Prophets, and Rabbis, who preserved for us the Holy Scriptures, knew that a time of trouble would come upon the world "such as never was since there was a nation " They prayed that The Messiah would come in their day. They believed in the coming of The Messiah. Do we, the Jews of this day, believe in the coming of the Messiah? I am afraid not many of us do. And unfortunately neither do most of our religious leaders. There was a time when the Holy Scriptures were studied and we Jews believed in the coming of The Messiah. **The Talmud, the Targums, the Midrashim, and the Prayer Books** reveal this fact. But because *He has tarried,* according to man's calculations, we have lost hope.

How will The Messiah come and what is the purpose of His coming? Let us read the Holy Scriptures, "For, behold the

Lord will come with fire, and with His chariots like a
whirlwind, to render His anger with fury, and His rebuke with
flames of fire. For by fire and by His sword will the Lord plead
with all flesh; and the slain of the Lord will be many." Isaiah
66:15,16. This means, that when The Messiah comes the
wicked will be destroyed. He comes to "plead with all flesh,"
and the living wicked will perish. This is what awaits the
ungodly. What becomes of the living holy and righteous
people? They will be redeemed and not see death. Look at this
promise concerning God's people: "And at that time shall
Michael [The Messiah] stand up, the great prince,which
standeth for the children of thy people: there shall be a time of
trouble, such as never was since there was a nation even to that
same time: and at that time thy people shall be delivered, every
one that shall be found written in the book. And many of them
that sleep in the dust of the earth shall awake, some to
everlasting life, and some to everlasting contempt." Daniel
12:1, 2.

The Bible teaches that the holy and righteous will be
resurrected at the coming of The Messiah. The Prophet Ezekiel
states: "... Thus saith the Lord God; Behold I will open your
graves, and cause you to come up out of your graves, and bring
you unto the land of Israel. And you shall know that I am the
Lord, when I open your graves, O My people, and brought you
out of your graves." Ezekiel 37:12,13.   Concerning the
righteous who have died before the coming of The Messiah, a
Midrashic comment says: "For what purpose will the royal
Messiah come, and what will he do? He will come to assemble
the exiles of Israel." Midrash Rabbah on Genesis 12: 12:12
chapter 98, section 9, Soncino Press. A Talmudic Rabbi said
that God holds in His hands certain keys, one of which is "the
key of the revival of the dead, for it is written, and ye shall
know that I am the Lord, when I have opened your graves
[Ezek. xxxvii, 13]." Ta'anith 2b, p. 3, Soncino Press.

The belief in the resurrection of the dead is a long-
cherished tenet of Jewish faith. Article 13 of the Thirteen
Principles of the Faith reads: "I believe with perfect faith that
there will be a resurrection of the dead at the time when it shall
please the Creator, blessed be His name, and exalted be the
remembrance of Him for ever and ever." Daily Prayers, p.167,
Dr. A. Th. Phillips, Hebrew Publishing Company. The Prayer
Book abounds in praise of God for the assurance given in the
Holy Scriptures that He will raise the dead to life. One such

statement reads: "Inscribe us in the Book of Life, for Thine own sake, O living God"; and, "Thou quickenest the dead, Thou art mighty to save." **Ibid.** p.217. "There is none but Thee, O our Redeemer, for the days of the Messiah; neither is there any like unto Thee, O our Saviour, for the resurrection of the dead." **Ibid.** p.321.

It is evident that when the **Targums, Talmud, and Midrashim** were written there were Jewish teachers who believed and taught the Biblical doctrine of the coming of The Messiah and the resurrection of the dead. We should be ever thankful to God for these precious revelations He has given to us through His prophets. We read further concerning the Lord's plans for the faithful believers in His written word: "For behold, I create new heavens and a new earth; and the former things shall not be remembered, nor come into mind. But be ye glad and rejoice for ever in that which I create; for, behold I create Jerusalem a rejoicing, and her people a joy. And I will rejoice in Jerusalem, and joy in My people; and the voice of weeping shall be no more heard in her, nor the voice of crying... The wolf and the lamb shall feed together, and the lion shall eat straw like the ox; and dust shall be the serpent's food. They shall not hurt nor destroy in all My holy mountain, saith the Lord." Isaiah 65:17-19, 25. "For as the new heavens and the new earth, which I will make, shall remain before Me, saith the Lord, so shall your seed and your name remain. And it shall come to pass, that from one new moon to another, and from one Sabbath to another, shall all flesh come to worship before Me, saith the Lord." Isaiah 66:22, 23. "From of old men have not heard, nor perceived by the ear, neither hath the eye seen a God beside Thee, who worketh for him that waiteth for Him." Isaiah 64:3.

This is a part of the wonderful plan which the Lord has revealed concerning the world to come. This will be the eternal home of those who give themselves fully to God, and have experienced what King David knew when he prayed, "Create in me a clean heart O God." Psalm 51:12. Those who by divine grace obey God's Ten Commandments and observe the seventh-day Sabbath, who seek both physically and spiritually to be ready for The Messiah's coming will be blessed by God. Let us read and meditate on this petition found in one of the widely used Prayer Books: "May it be Thy will, Lord our God and God of our fathers, that we keep Thy laws in this world, and thus be worthy to live to see and share the happiness and blessing in the Messianic days and in the life of the world to come." **Daily Prayer Book,** pp. 133, 540, Phillip Birnbaum, Hebrew Publishing Company. May God help each one of us to keep His holy law, to follow His Holy Bible, and to so live that we may be ready when He comes. With this statement from the Talmud we close this chapter: "R. Hiyya b. Abba said in T. Johanan's name: 'All the prophets prophesied (all the good things) only in respect to the Messianic era; but ask for the world to come, the eye hath not seen, O Lord, beside Thee, what He hath prepared for him that waiteth for Him.'" **Sanhedrin** 99a, volume 2, p. 670.

CHAPTER 2

The Messiah—Do We Need Him?

Many people ask the question, Why do we need a Messiah? Why do we talk about The Messiah's coming? If He should come, what good would it do? What is the purpose of His coming? These questions are asked by skeptics, and also by godly people because of their sincere desire to know. Nearly 3,500 years have passed since the people of Israel first became a nation. During these many centuries devout Jews generally cherished God's promise of the coming of The Messiah. *The reason why we find it taught in the Targums, the Talmud, the Midrashim, and the Prayer Books is because it has been set forth in the Holy Scriptures by Moses and the Prophets.* Today in this age of widespread disregard for law and order much skepticism prevails even among our Jewish people concerning that Messianic promise in the Word of God. It is no wonder then that people often ask, Why do we need a Messiah?

The Hebrew teachers who prepared the original Prayer Book in days of old have recorded some remarkable expressions of hope for The Messiah's coming. "Speedily cause the Offspring of Thy servant David to flourish, and let his glory be exalted by Thy help, for we hope for Thy deliverance all day." **Daily Prayer Book,** pp. 90, 206, Philip Birnbaum, Hebrew Publishing Company. Another such expression of desire for the coming of The Messiah is stated thus in the **Yigdal**: "At time's end He will send our Messiah to save all who wait for his final help. God, in His great mercy, will revive the dead; blessed be His name forever." **Ibid.,** p. 14. How wonderful it would be if all our Jewish people would believe in, and talk about, the coming of The Messiah as earnestly as did the original writers of those passages in the Prayer Book! Here is another expression of the longing for The Messiah's coming: "May it be Thy will, Lord our God and God of our fathers, that we keep Thy laws in this world, and thus be worthy to live to see and share the happiness and blessing in the Messianic days and in the life of the world to come." **Ibid.,** pp. 134, 540. These statements set forth the ancient Bible doctrine that The Messiah will come and that He will reward the faithful with eternal life, happiness, and blessing in the world to come.

"The Thirteen Articles of Faith formulated according to Maimonides in his Mishnah Commentary to **Sanhedrin,** introduction to Chapter IX which have been accepted by the great majority of Jews and are found in the prayer book" presents this as the twelfth: "I firmly believe in the coming of the Messiah; and although He may tarry, I daily hope for his coming." **The Jewish Encyclopedia,** volume 2, p. 151, article **"Articles of Faith."** That affirmation of faith in the Biblical doctrine of the coming of The Messiah is clearly stated in many prayer books. The teachers of our Hebrew people down through the ages have believed in the literal coming of The Messiah. In **The Authorized Prayer Book,** revised edition, by Dr. Joseph Hertz, formerly Chief Rabbi of the British Empire, we are told: "The salvation of the individual Israelite is linked with the salvation of Israel; and through Israel, with the triumph of righteousness in the coming of the Messianic Kingdom. To the overwhelming majority of the House of Israel in every generation, the Messianic Hope has meant the belief in the coming of the Messiah (literally 'the Anointed One') an exalted Personality, upon whom shall rest the Spirit of the Lord." p. 254, Bloch Publishing Company.

The Talmud states what one distinguished Rabbi believed concerning the coming of The Messiah: "Rabbi Johanan said: When you see a generation ever dwindling, hope for him [The Messiah], as it is written. When the enemy shall come in like a flood, the Spirit of the Lord shall lift up a standard against him, which is followed by, And the redeemer shall come to Zion (Isaiah 59: 19, 20)." **Sanhedrin** 98a, volume 2, p. 663, Soncino Press. It is certainly clear that our Jewish fathers all emphasized their belief in the coming of The Messiah to save His people. They knew that The Messiah would be a great personality, and that He would come to put down the forces of evil and rule the world with a scepter of righteousness.

"In the beginning God created the heaven and the earth." "And God saw everything that He had made and, behold, it was very good." Genesis 1:1, 31. How did God create this world? He created it very good. "God made man upright." Ecclesiastes 7:29. There was no sin in the universe until the rebellion of Lucifer. He was cast out into the earth with the evil angels who had rallied to his side. In this world we find that Satan with his cohorts was ready to lead man into sin.

Lucifer, having debased himself, became the devil called Satan, and tempted Eve in the Garden of Eden. Regarding the temptation, the Torah states: "Now the serpent was more subtle than any beast of the field which the Lord God had made. And he said unto the woman, Yea, hath God said, Ye shall not eat of every tree of the garden? And the woman said unto the serpent, We may eat of the fruit of the trees of the garden: but of the fruit of the tree which is in the midst of the garden God hath said, Ye shall not eat of it, neither shall ye touch it, lest ye die. And the serpent said unto the woman, Ye shall not surely die: for God doth know that in the day ye eat thereof, then your eyes shall be opened, and ye shall be as gods, knowing good and evil. And when the woman saw that the tree was good for food, and that it was pleasant to the eyes, and a tree to be desired to make one wise, she took of the fruit thereof, and did eat, and gave also unto her husband with her; and he did eat." Genesis 3:1-6.

Originally, the serpent was a remarkable creature. The Bible says that it was more subtle than any of the other animal creatures which God had created. Satan chose this creature as his medium through which to deceive Eve. He had waited until she would be alone. When she was walking through the garden and came to the tree of knowledge of good and evil, there was the serpent in the tree. As Eve passed by the tree of knowledge of good and evil, she heard a voice and she looked up and saw the serpent. It spoke to her and said: "Yea, hath God said, Ye shall not eat of every tree of the garden?" Eve answered: "We may eat of the fruit of the trees of the garden: but of the fruit of the tree which is in the midst of the garden, God hath said, Ye shall not eat of it, neither shall ye touch it, lest ye die." verses 2, 3. According to Genesis 2:17, the Lord had said to Adam and Eve: "But of the tree of the knowledge of good and evil, thou shalt not eat of it; for in the day that thou eatest thereof thou shalt surely die." The last part of that passage in Hebrew literally reads: "Because that in the day of thy eating from it dying thou shalt die." In the **Midrash Rabbah**, on Genesis, chapter 16, section 6, volume 1, p. 131, we find the comment that "[this intimated] death for Adam and Eve, and death for his descendants." Editorial footnote No. 5 on the same page remarks: "This is deduced from the doubling of the verb, which as usual is understood as an extension." What does this mean? It does not mean that they would die immediately after eating the forbidden fruit, but rather that a gradual deterioration of the

life forces would ensue in the process of aging. Until they
sinned by disobeying God, Adam and Eve had free access to
the tree of life and its fruit, which was an antidote against
sickness and death. Thus they could enjoy a perpetual bloom
of youth, vigor, and eternally good health. But when they
failed to stand the test of loyalty to God, they were expelled
from the Edenic home, and cherubim, with a flaming sword
which turned every way, guarding every access to the life
giving tree. This was done by directive from God, "Lest he
[sinful man] put forth his hand, and take also of the tree of life,
and eat, and live forever." Genesis 3:22-24. By this means the
Lord made it impossible for man to live forever in his sinful
condition and be a perpetual agent of evil. Thus, by their
refusal to obey God's moral law, given for the preservation and
perpetuation of the human race, mankind forfeited the right to
everlasting life. Death, is both the natural consequence of sin
and the ultimate penalty for persistent impenitence.

The question of primary importance is this: <u>what is the
remedy for sin?</u> How can man regain the priceless heritage that
was his by creation and lost by sin? This is where The
Messiah's role is an essential part of God's intervention to save
man from his lost condition. From their study of the Holy
Scriptures our devout teachers in ages past understood more
than many can imagine about the significance of the coming of
the promised Messiah. We are living, according to Bible
prophecy, in the time of the end—the period preceding the
advent of The Messiah to reign in glory over the earth. Sooner
than many think, He will come. However, before the lost
Paradise can be regained, we must do our part in getting ready
to have a part in The Messiah's kingdom. In order to do this,
we must understand what our proper relationship to Him and
God should be. Concerning the time of The Messiah's
appearing, the Lord has said: "In that day, saith the Lord, will I
assemble her that halteth, and I will gather her that is driven
away, and her that I have afflicted; I will make her that halted a
remnant, and her that was cast far off a mighty nation; and the
Lord shall reign over them in Mount Zion from thenceforth
even for ever." Micah 4:6, 7.

I want to be a citizen of that everlasting kingdom of the
world to come! What about you? As you read the rest of this
chapter you will understand what God requires of us in order
that we might be citizens of that eternal kingdom. We know
from the study of the Torah, as well as the balance of the Holy

Scriptures, that the violation of God's great moral law—The Ten Commandments—is sin, disobedience to God. That is why on the Day of Atonement, the blood of the Lord's goat, as related in Leviticus 16, was shed for making atonement for the sins of Israel. The blood was taken by the high priest into the holy of holies of the Sanctuary [Temple] and there sprinkled seven times before the ark of the covenant. Why? Because inside that ark were the Ten Commandments engraved by the finger of God on two tables of stone—the very law which the people had transgressed. Thus sin is the transgression of God's law. Why was an atonement necessary? Because death is the penalty that the sinner incurs by transgressing God's holy law. We have seen that such was the penalty incurred by Adam and Eve when they sinned. It is the penalty that every person incurs when he transgresses the law of God. "The soul that sinneth, it shall die." Ezekiel 18: 4, 20. All men are under the death penalty, "for there is no man that sinneth not." 1 Kings 8:46; 2 Chronicles 6:36. "For there is not a righteous man upon earth that doeth good, and sinneth not." Ecclesiastes 7:20.

We have a God who is great in love and mercy to His erring children. To Moses on Mount Sinai, the Lord proclaimed: "...The Lord, the Lord God, merciful and gracious, long-suffering, and abundant in goodness and truth; keeping mercy unto the thousandth generation, <u>forgiving iniquity and transgression and sin; and that will by no means clear the guilty;</u>..." Exodus 34:6,7. That statement recorded in the Torah shows that God, in His love and mercy, has provided a way whereby He can pardon the sinner and yet be just in doing it. Moses was given by God a detailed illustration of the divinely appointed plan for salvation of the repentant sinner.

When Adam and Eve sinned, they immediately found themselves naked, deprived of the vestment of glory with which they were clothed in their original innocence and holiness. After calling the guilty pair to account for their evil-doing and promising that in the future the seed of the woman would deal a death blow to the adversary to whose dominion they had submitted, "the Lord God made for Adam and his wife garments of skins and clothed them." Genesis 3:2. This first mention of "skins" in the Bible indicates that some animals had been slain in order to provide a covering to hide the nakedness and shame of the world's first human transgressors of God's law. Later Cain and Abel, the first two sons of Adam and Eve, came to worship before the Lord.

"Cain brought of the fruit of the ground an offering unto the Lord. And Abel, he also brought of the firstlings of his flock and of the fat thereof. And the Lord had respect unto Abel and to his offering; but unto Cain and to his offering He had not respect." Genesis 4:3-5. The offering of Cain was rejected, while that of Abel was accepted. Why? What did all that ancient ritual of animal sacrifices mean? We find it observed by Noah, Abraham, Isaac, Jacob, and Job, and later, on a more extensive and elaborate scale, by Israel. What was the purpose of it? *Let me explain!* The penalty for sin is death. By transgressing God's law, man forfeits his right to live. The ancient ritual of sacrifices served as an object lesson for making known, by way of illustration, God's plan for saving the repentant sinner from the penalty and power of sin. Because death is the penalty for sin, the sinner's life must be required of him to meet the demands of divine justice. Hence the slaying of the kid or lamb, brought and offered as a sin-offering, illustrated the atonement made by God's redemptive provision for the salvation of every truly repentant sinner. Concerning the atonement, we are told: "It is related to i.e. enduring the full penalty of the offense, and to satisfaction, i.e. rendering a full legal equivalent for the wrong done." **The Universal Jewish Encyclopedia**, volume 1, p. 61, article "Atonement."

How could the slaying of a kid or a lamb and the sprinkling of its blood before the violated law of God render to Him "a full legal equivalent for the wrong done?" A distinguished, keen-minded Rabbi has said: "It is most difficult for us to understand how the sprinkling of blood and the smoke of burning animal suet can influence the will of God...Even more difficult to comprehend is how the burnt offerings possess automatic expiating power." Because death is the penalty for sin, the Lord said concerning the animal sacrifice that "the life of the flesh is in the blood; and I have given it to you upon the altar to make atonement for your souls; for it is the blood that maketh atonement by reason of the life." Leviticus 17:11. Sages of the Talmudic times of long ago acknowledged this fact: "Surely atonement can be made only with the blood, as it says, For it is the blood that maketh atonement by reason of the life." **Zebahim** 6a ,pp. 24, 25. Furthermore, in the ancient object lesson of the system of animal sacrifices the shedding of the animal's blood was symbolic. "The sacrifice cleanses only through the blood that is sprinkled, the blood symbolizing the

THE MESSIAH—DO WE NEED HIM? 21

life of the one sacrificing, which but for the substitution of the victim, would have to be surrendered in expiation of the sin (Zeb. 6a.)."**The Jewish Encyclopedia,** volume 10, p. 625, article, "**Sacrifice.**"

It should be clear that Cain's offering of the fruit of the ground was not acceptable to God. It might serve as a thank offering, but not as a sin offering to atone for his sins. But there was no substitutionary shedding of blood, no vicarious sacrifice of an animal's life, in Cain's offering. There was such in Abel's, and for this reason it was acceptable to the Lord. In his hatred for his righteous brother, Cain added to his sin of disobedience [Genesis 4:7] the murder of his own brother [verses 8-11]. It is God's requirement that blood be shed in the ancient system of animal sacrifices for the atonement of sin, which constituted a very important part of the ritual of the Sanctuary [Temple] services in Israel. Is it mystifying and puzzling? Could a man guilty of having robbed and killed another person repent of it later and satisfactorily settle the case with the Judge of all the earth by confessing his guilt and offering to Him the carcass of a little goat or lamb? Would a modern court of Justice pardon and set free a self-confessed criminal in return for the dead body of a domestic animal of so little market value? It is here where one of the roles of The Messiah is played in the divinely appointed plan for man's redemption from sin. This Jewish [Biblical] concept of vicarious or substitutionary atonement is not new. "The use of blood in sacrifice appears to follow a principle that the blood of the animal is a substitute for the lives of those who make the sacrifice. 'I have given it [the blood] to you upon the altar to make atonement for your souls: for it is the blood that maketh atonement by reason of the life' [Lev. 17:11]. If it were not for the pouring out or sprinkling of animal blood, the ancient Hebrews believed, they themselves would be slain. Thus the blood of a lamb was smeared on the lintels during the plague of the death of the first-born, to protect the inhabitants of the house against death [Ex. 12:22]. "-**The Universal Jewish Encyclopedia,** volume. 2, p. 406, article, "**Blood.**" "In every sacrifice there is the idea of substitution; the victim takes the place of the human sinner. The laying of hands upon the victim's head is an ordinary rite by which the substitution and the transfer of sins are effected. . . . The sprinkling of the blood is essential to all sin offerings. By dipping the finger in the victim's blood and applying it to a sacred object like the

altar, the priest re-establishes the union between the people that
he represents and the Deity."-**The Jewish Encyclopedia**,
volume 2, p. 286, article "**Atonement.**" "No man can by any
means redeem his brother, nor give to God a ransom for him —
for too costly is the redemption of their soul." Psalm 49:8, 9.
No, not even the dearest of family ties can provide a ransom for
the sinner's soul. Why? "The soul that sinneth, it shall die.
The son shall not bear the iniquity of the father, neither shall
the father bear the iniquity of the son." Ezekiel 18:20. That is,
not even our closest relative, however willing he might be to
save us , cannot serve as our sinbearer.

The God of Israel has provided a Redeemer for us and has
promised that He should come: "A Redeemer will come to
Zion, and unto them that turn from transgression in Israel, saith
the Lord." Isaiah 59:20. The promised Redeemer was to come
to Zion —to the people of Israel; but not to all those in Israel
— only to those who turn from transgression. Earlier in this
chapter, we have shown that in the Talmud it was taught that
the prophecy in Isaiah "that a Redeemer would come to Zion"
was to be fulfilled in the coming of The Messiah. In a later
chapter, we shall consider the manner in which He would
ransom the penitent who turn from transgression in Israel.
Now we shall notice what the ultimate results of His
redemptive work will be in behalf of such truly repentant souls.
Here are promised the results of our redemption by Him: "I
will ransom them from the power of the grave; I will redeem
them from death." Hosea 13:14. Shortly afterward this,
assurance was given: "Thy dead men shall live, together with
my dead body shall they arise. Awake and sing, ye that dwell
in the dust; for thy dew is as the dew of herbs, and the earth
shall cast out the dead. For, behold, the Lord cometh out of
His place to punish the inhabitants of the earth for their
iniquity." Isaiah 26:9. Long before that promise was written,
the Psalmist said, in praise to God: "As for me, I will behold
Thy face in righteousness: I shall be satisfied, when I awake,
with Thy likeness." Psalm 17:15. So in the great resurrection
day, at The Messiah's advent to reign over His people, all the
redeemed will be restored - recreated by the miracle of the
resurrection of the dead — to the likeness of their Maker.

Job, that faithful servant of God about 37 centuries ago, in
his great physical affliction, declared his faith in the coming of
the promised Redeemer: "I know that my Redeemer liveth, and
that He shall stand at the latter day upon the earth: and after

they have thus destroyed my skin, yet in my flesh shall I see God: whom I shall see for myself, and mine eyes shall behold, and not another; though my reins be consumed within me." Job 19:25-27. Thus the doctrine of the resurrection of the dead in the last day is a Biblical one. It will take place at the time when The Messiah shall come for the final deliverance of His people. This blessed hope has been cherished to the end of his days by many a faithful Israelite now sleeping in the dust of the earth. This is what is taught in Ezekiel 37:1-14 and Daniel 12:1-3. Yes! The Messiah is coming for two purposes: (1) to reward the righteous and holy people by delivering them for eternity; and (2) to punish the wicked by putting them all to death. In the world to come, there will be no more sin or sinners because all sinners will have been destroyed. There will be no more Satan and his wicked angels and followers to tempt us, for they, too, will be destroyed in that fire which God shall bring upon the earth to destroy sin and sinners forever. Thus evil will never rise up again. "For, behold, the Lord will come with fire, and with His chariots like a whirlwind, to render His anger with fury, and His rebuke with flames of fire. For by fire and by His sword will the Lord plead with all flesh: and the slain of the Lord shall be many." Isaiah 66:15,16. What we do to get ready to meet The Messiah, we must do quickly.

The Holy Scriptures [the Bible] tells us that God is going to put an end to all sin: "What do ye imagine against the Lord? He will make an utter end: affliction shall not rise up the second time." Nahum 1:9. In Ezekiel 18:30-32 we read these words: "Therefore I will judge you, O house of Israel, every one according to his ways, saith the Lord God. Repent, and turn yourselves from all your transgressions, whereby ye have transgressed; and make you a new heart and a new spirit: for why will ye die, O house of Israel: For I have no pleasure in the death of him that dieth, saith the Lord God: wherefore turn yourselves, and live ye." Here we find that the Lord is going to judge the people. He is asking us to repent and turn from our transgressions so that iniquity (sin) will not be our ruin. He pleads with us to cast away our sins, and then He adds, "For why will ye die, O house of Israel: For I have no pleasure in the death of him that dieth." God has no pleasure in anyone's dying. That is the purpose of sending The Messiah — to save man from eternal death. God wants to save them from death— for eternal life. That is why He says, "Wherefore turn yourselves and live." Turn away from sin, turn to righteousness and live for eternity. The reward of the redeemed is found in Isaiah 65:17, 19, and 25 : "For behold, I create new heavens and a new earth: and the former shall not be remembered, nor come into mind. But be ye glad and rejoice for ever in that which I create: for, behold, I create Jerusalem a rejoicing, and her people a joy. And I will rejoice in Jerusalem, and joy in My people: and the voice of weeping shall be no more heard in her, nor the voice of crying...The wolf and the lamb shall feed together, and the lion shall eat straw like the bullock; and dust shall be the serpent's meat. They shall not hurt nor destroy in all My holy mountain." This is the reward of the holy and righteous people. We have this precious promise; "For as the new heavens and the new earth, which I will make, shall remain before Me, saith the Lord, so shall your seed and your name remain. And it shall come to pass, that from one new moon to another, and from one Sabbath to another, shall all flesh come to worship before Me, saith the Lord." Isaiah 66:22, 23.

CHAPTER 3

WHO IS THE JEWISH MESSIAH?

The age old question, "Who Is the Jewish Messiah?" has been asked by many of our Jewish people. Our purpose is to find out what God has said concerning this in the Holy Scriptures. "Who hath ascended up into heaven, and descended? Who hath gathered the wind in his fists? Who hath bound the water in his garment? Who hath established all the ends of the earth? What is his name, and what is his son's name, if thou knowest?" Proverbs 30:4. Several questions are asked here with reference to the creation of our world and the last is concerning the Creator. *"What is His name, and what is His Son's name, if thou knowest?" Does this refer to the true God? Does it mean that God has a Son?*

The next Bible text for our study is: "Know thou and understand thou: From the going forth of a commandment to restore and to rebuild Jerusalem unto Prince Messiah [shall be] seven weeks and sixty-two weeks." Daniel 9:25. Some renderings of this text give "Messiah the Prince." The word "anointed" is **Mashiach** in Hebrew, which is rendered as either "anointed" or "Messiah." Here God calls the Prince The Messiah. Let us read Daniel 12:1, 2 : "And at that time shall Michael stand up, the great prince which standeth for the children of thy people: and there shall be a time of trouble such as never was since there was a nation even to that same time: and at that time thy people shall be delivered, every one that shall be found written in the book. And many of them that sleep in the dust of earth shall awake." Notice that "at that time shall Michael stand up, the great prince." In the **Babylonia Talmud** it is stated that "the Prince of the Universe said to Him [God]: 'Sovereign of the Universe!' It [the earth] both fulfilled Thy desire [for songs of praise] on behalf of this righteous man [King Hezekiah]." **Sanhedrin** 94a, volume 2, p. 63, Soncino Press. An editorial footnote comments on the expression "the Prince of the Universe" by saying: "This is a special angel set over the world, distinct from the guardian angels of the separate nations. He has been identified with Metatron;" etc. - Ibid. **The Jewish Encyclopedia** says that

"Targ. Yer, to Ex. xxiv. 1 has Michael instead of Metatron. . . .
The early commentators with good reason identified the prince
of the world (Hul. 60a; Zeb. 16b; Sanh. 94a) with Metatron. . . .
While, as noted above, Targ. Yer. to Ex. xxiv 1 substitutes the
name of Michael for Metatron, which is found in the other
sources." -volume 8, p. 519, article "**Metatron.**" The same
work points out that "the prophets developed the hope of an
ideal Messianic future through the reign of a son of the house
of David"; and in doing so it cites the fact that "in Dan. xii. 2
the resurrection is extended to both the wicked and the
righteous: the latter 'shall awake to everlasting life,' the former
'to shame and everlasting horror' (A. V. 'contempt')." volume 5,
p. 209, article "**Eschatology.**"

Dr. Judah B. Slotki, in comment on Daniel 12, correctly
remarks: "This chapter is generally taken by Jewish authorities
to refer to the remote future which will herald the advent of the
Messianic era." **Daniel, Ezra, Nehemiah,** pp. 100, 101
Soncino Press. If God calls The Messiah "the Prince," and
Michael is called "the Great Prince," then Michael would be
another name for The Messiah. Let us look at the Hebrew
word **Mika'el,** the English of which is "Michael." This is a
compound of three Hebrew words: (a) **mi,** which means "who"
or "he who" (b); **ka,** which means "as" or "like"; and (c) **'El,**
which means "God." Thus the Messiah's name "Michael" is
understood literally to mean "He who (is) like God."
Furthermore, to show that this is The Messiah to whom God is
referring, He calls him "Michael, the great prince." Now
observe the last part of the verse, "and at that time thy people
shall be delivered." We recognize that when The Messiah
comes, He is to deliver the people of God. That is why in the
**Jewish Prayer Books, the Talmud and the Midrash
Rabbah,** we read that the Son of David, The Messiah, The
Redeemer, The Deliverer, would ransom God's people. The
fact that Michael is called the Prince and also the one who is to
deliver the people, shows that this text refers to the Messiah's
coming. Still further, is it not a fact that the one who is to raise
the righteous dead from their graves is The Messiah? This
thought is emphasized in verse 2: "And many of them that
sleep in the dust of the earth shall awake." Another point to
consider is that God is the King. Notice Psalm 47:8 "For God
is the King of all the earth." Yes, He is the King not only of
this earth but of the entire universe. Since He is the King, how
logical that the Prince is The Messiah! Is not the relationship

of the Prince to the King that of son to father? Since God is the King and Messiah is the Prince, therefore The Messiah is the Son of the King.

"Who hath ascended up into heaven, and descended? Who hath gathered the wind in his fists? Who hath bound the waters in his garment? Who hath established all the ends of the earth? What is his name, and what is his son's name, if thou knowest?{ Proverbs 30: 4-6. Observe that God asked three important questions: **(a) Who created the world? (b) What is His name? (c) And what is His son's name?** Concerning the name of the Creator, in the Hebrew Bible the specific name of God is YHWH **(Yahweh or Yahveh).** However, this name has been mistakenly rendered by some English translators as **Jehovah.** In the eighth century the Masoretic scholars added the vowel points to the Hebrew Bible text. Since the Jewish people considered the divine name YHWH too sacred to be pronounced, the Masorites gave to YHWH the vowel points belonging to 'DNI Adonai (Lord). As a result of this, when our Jewish people, in reading aloud the Hebrew Scriptures, come to the name of YHWH, they do not pronounce it as such but instead they say 'DNI (Adonai). The Midrashic teachers apply Proverbs 30:4-6 to our God and to His son — Israel — in Exodus 42:2. "It is said of the Lord: What is His name? (Prov. loc. cit.) 'Rock' is His name, 'Almighty' is His name, 'Lord of Hosts' is His name: And what is His son's name, if thou knowest? (Pro. loc. cit.) 'Israel is My son, My first-born' (Exod. IV, 22)." -**Midrash Rabbah,** on Numbers,   volume 1, chapter 12, section 11, p. 479, Soncino Press. In this excerpt the word "son" is applied to Israel as it is in Exodus 4:22. But this calls for fuller consideration. "The Holy One, Blessed be He, told Moses: Just as I have made Jacob a firstborn, for it says: Israel is My son, My firstborn (id. iv, 22), so will I make the King Messiah a firstborn, as it says: I also will appoint him firstborn (Ps. LXXXIX: 28)." -**Midrash Rabah**, on Exodus, chapter 19,section 7, pp. 237-238, Soncino Press.   The reference in Psalm 2:7 "thou art My son," refers to an individual, not to a people. The Talmudic record states: "Our Rabbis taught, the Holy One, blessed be He, will say to the Messiah, the son of David (May he reveal himself speedily in our days!). 'Ask of Me anything, and I will give it to thee, as it is said, I will tell of the decree, etc. this day have I begotten thee'," etc.-**Sukkah** 52a, p. 247, Soncino Press. Concerning the Son's name, we read: "Behold the Lord hath proclaimed unto the end of the earth; say ye to the daughter of Zion: 'Behold, thy salvation cometh; behold, His reward is with Him, and His recompense before Him.' And they shall call them Thy holy people, The redeemed of the Lord." Isaiah 62:11,12.

In the Scripture passage, the Hebrew noun rendered in English as "salvation" is **yesha'**, singular in number and masculine in gender. It is used 36 times in the Hebrew Scriptures and is translated into English as "salvation" 32 times, the four exceptions being "safety" (in Job 5:4, 11; Psalm 12:6) and "saving" (in Psalm 20:7). However, the proclamation says: "Behold, thy salvation cometh. His reward is with Him, and His recompense before Him." Isaiah 62:11. The words "Him" (twice) certainly imply, beyond any doubt, that a divine Saviour brings that "salvation" with Him when He comes to give to men their reward and recompense. That "salvation" **(yesha')**, according to many Bible prophecies, is to be brought by The Messiah, whose name is Yeshua - "Salvation of the Lord" — as we have indicated previously. So God has not only revealed to us that The Messiah is His Son, but also the Hebrew name of The Messiah. Consider this statement: "Why are the nations in an uproar? And why do the peoples mutter in vain? The kings of the earth stand up, and the rulers take counsel together against the Lord, and against His anointed: let us break their bands asunder and cast away their cords from us. He that sitteth in heaven laugheth, the Lord hath them in derision. Then will He speak unto them in His wrath, and affright them in His sore displeasure: truly it is I that have established My king upon Zion, My holy mountain. I will tell of the decree: The Lord said unto me: 'Thou art My son, This day have I begotten thee. Ask of Me, and I will give the nations for thine inheritance, and the ends of the earth for thy possession. Thou shalt break them with a rod of iron; thou shalt dash them in pieces like a potter's vessel.'" Psalm 2:1-9. The word "Lord" is the English rendering for the tetragrammaton in the Hebrew text. Further, the Hebrew word mashiach rendered as "anointed" in the English text of Psalm 2:2 can just as consistently be translated as "Messiah."

There are some particular words in the Hebrew that will enable us more easily to understand them. "Why are the **goyim** in an uproar? And why do the peoples mutter in vain? The kings of the earth stand up, and the rulers take counsel together against the Lord, and against his Messiah: 'Let us break their bands asunder, and cast away their cords from us.' He that sitteth in Heaven laugheth, the Lord ['Adonai] hath them in derision. Then will He speak unto them in His wrath, and affright them in His sore displeasure: 'Truly it is I that have established My king upon Zion, My holy mountain'." Now The Messiah speaks: "I will tell of the decree: The Lord [YHWH] said unto me: Thou art My son." Notice how distinctly the Bible makes it clear that in this text the Lord is the Father, for we find Him saying to The Messiah: "Thou art My Son, this day have I begotten thee." We know that this refers to The Messiah, because the latter part of the second verse reads that "the kings of the earth stand up, and the rulers take counsel together, against the Lord and against His Mashiach [Messiah, "Anointed One"]." This entire chapter is dealing with the Lord, the Father, and with the "Anointed One," The Messiah, who is His Son. Psalm 2 predicted the determined opposition which The Messiah, the Son of God, would meet, and yet it foretells His triumph over His enemies. We read in verses 7 to 9 "Thou art My son, this day have I begotten thee. Ask of Me, and I will give the nations [goyim] for thine inheritance, and the ends of the earth for thy possession. Thou shalt break them with a rod of iron; thou shalt dash them in pieces like a potter's vessel." We ask again, Who is this 'son' spoken of here? Some commentators have suggested that the 'son' in Psalm 2 refers to David; others say it refers to Solomon, David's son. But this scripture says, "Blessed are all they that put their trust in Him." Verse 12. God has never told us to put our trust in any human being, whether it be in David, in Solomon, or in any other person. Indeed, He forbids us to place our confidence in mortal man. He says: *"Cursed is the man that trusted in man, and maketh flesh his arm."* Jeremiah 17:5.

We read in the *Talmud* about the meaning of the expression; "Against the Lord and against His anointed" (Verse 2):" 'Against God and His Messiah' as it is said, Why are the nations in an uproar, and why do the peoples mutter in vain, etc." -'Abodah Zarah 3b, p. 9, Soncino Press. The Scripture passage quoted from Psalm 2 is really a wonderful prophetic preview of The Messiah and His work. It is very evident, then, that this Psalm refers to a divine person, the King (verse 6); also to The Messiah (verse 2), the Son of God (verse 7), who eventually will inherit the heathen and the uttermost parts of the earth for His possession (verse 8), the one who merits our trust (verse 12). In the Hebrew text of Psalm 2, our God is

called 'Adonai which in the English translation is rendered
"Lord." "[As regards] The Messiah — it is written: And this is
the name whereby he shall be called, The Lord is our
righteousness." -Baba Bathra 75b,p 303, Soncino Press. The
Scripture quoted is Jeremiah 23:6. "What is the name of King
Messiah? Rabbi Abba b. Kahana said: His name is 'the Lord';
as it is written: 'And this is the name whereby he shall be
called, the Lord is our righteousness' (Jer. xxiii, 6)." -Midrash
Rabbah, on Lamentations, chapter 1, section 16, part 51, pp.
135, 136, Soncino Press.

David, the sweet singer of Israel, recognized a compound
unity in the Godhead when, by inspiration of God, he wrote
Psalm 110, which says: "The Lord [YHWH] saith unto my
Lord ['Adoni]: 'Sit thou at My right hand, until I make thine
enemies thy footstool. The rod of thy strength the Lord will
send out of Zion: 'Rule thou in the midst of thine enemies.'
Thy people offer themselves willingly in the day of thy
warfare; in adornments of holiness, from the womb of the
dawn, thine is the dew of thy youth. The Lord hath sworn, and
will not repent: 'Thou art a priest for ever after the manner of
Melchizedek.' The Lord ['Adonai] at thy right hand doth
crush kings in the day of His wrath. He will judge among the
nations." Psalm 110:1-6 In this Psalm two Divine beings are
mentioned: "The Lord [YHWH]" and "My Lord ['Adonai]."
Usually the word "Lord" appears as 'Adonai in the Hebrew,
the plural form, but when the word "my" is used with it, it
takes the singular possessive form 'Adoni. The first line in the
English version reads: "The LORD saith unto my Lord." This
may not be easy to understand, but observe that the first
"LORD" is spelled with a large capital and three small capital
letters while the second "Lord" is spelled with only the first
letter a capital and the rest in small letters. What does that
mean? It means that when you read in the English Bible the
word "LORD" in one large and three small capital letters
corresponds to 'Adonai in the Hebrew text. Thus the English
rendering of the Hebrew in Psalm 110:1 is thus: "The LORD
[YHWH] saith unto my Lord ['Adoni]." The Hebrew shows
that two distinct persons are referred to in this text, each
bearing a Divine name. But of whom is the LORD speaking:
He is speaking to none other than The Messiah who, in this
text, is called "my Lord ['Adoni]."

In addition we read concerning Aaron's rod (staff):"That
same staff also is destined to be held in the hand of King

Messiah (may it be speedily in our day!); as it says, The staff of thy strength the Lord will send out to Zion: Rule thou in the midst of thine enemies. (Ps. cx, 2)." -**Midrash Rabbah,** on Numbers, chapter 18, sect. 23, volume 2, p.744, Soncino Press. In verse 4 the LORD says to The Messiah:"Thou art a priest for ever after the manner of Melchezedek." In Psalm 110:1-6 with the emphasis given in the Hebrew: "The LORD [YHWH], 'Sit thou at My right hand, until I make thine enemies thy footstool.' The rod of thy strength the Lord will send out of Zion: 'Rule thou in the midst of thine enemies.' Thy people offer themselves willingly in the day of thy warfare; in adornments of holiness, from the womb of the dawn, thine is the dew of thy youth. The Lord hath sworn, and He will not repent: 'Thou art a priest for ever after the manner of Melchizedek.' The Lord ['**Adonai**] at thy right hand doth crush kings in the day of His wrath. He will judge among the nations [**goyim**]."This Bible passage indicates that the Godhead is what may be properly called a uniplural or a compound unity, but not a sole or absolute unity. It is an *'echad* (unity), as stated in Deuteronomy 6:4, but not a *yachid* (a sole unity) as this latter Hebrew term denotes. It should be carefully noted that in the first verse the Lord says to the psalmist's Lord ('Adoni), The Messiah: "Sit thou on My right hand," i.e., in the position of authority, power, and honor next to that of the Lord Himself. Consider Proverbs 8:20-36. Notice that the term "wisdom" is personified. "Wisdom" is represented in *'echad* relationship to the Lord. Surely, then, this refers to The Messiah. What do we read in this text? In verse 22 The Messiah says:"The Lord possessed me in the beginning of His way before His works of old."Before the Lord ever made this world, The Messiah was in existence. Take notice of verses 23 to 25, "I was set up from everlasting, from the beginning, or ever the earth was. When there were no depths, I was brought forth; when there were no fountains abounding with water. Before the mountains were settled, before the hills was I brought forth."This preexistence of The Messiah is recognized by the ancient Jewish teachers in the Talmudic writings. In comment on Psalm 72:17, this is said: "The name of the Messiah, as it is written, His [sc, The Messiah's] name shall endure for ever, and has existed before the sun!-I will tell you: only its [the sun's] cavity was created before the world was created, but its fire [was created] on the eve of Sabbath." -**Pesachim** 54a , pp. 265, 266, Soncino Press.

These words in Proverbs 8:27 are very significant: "when He prepared the heavens, I was there."Notice verses 29, 30 also: "When He set to the sea its bound that the waters should not pass beyond its shores: when He appointed the foundations of the earth: then I was by Him, as one brought up with Him: and I was daily His delight, rejoicing always before Him." Proverbs 8, verse 32 : "Now therefore hearken unto me, O ye children: for blessed are they that keep my ways." Observe verse 33: "Hear instruction, and be wise, and refuse it not." Note verses 34 and 35: "Blessed is the man that heareth me, watching daily at my gates, waiting at the posts of my doors. For whoso findeth me findeth life, and shall obtain favor of the LORD."

Whoever finds the Messiah finds eternal life and blessed are they who enter into this wonder promise. This was the message of the prophets long ago. With God "is the foundation of life." Psalm 36:10. "In the way of righteousness is life." Proverbs 12:28. The person designated as Wisdom declared, "Whoso findeth Me findeth life." Proverbs 8:35. Yes, "even life forevermore." Psalm 133:3. The question may arise: Why is it that only a few find the truth? The answer to this question is that the majority do not take time to study God's Word in order to know what is truth, nor are they determined to accept it when they find it.

We have already read in Proverbs that the Messiah was with God during creation. Now let us read: "And God said, Let us make man in our image, after our likeness:...So God created man in His own image, in the image of God created He him; male and female created He them." Genesis 1:26, 26. To whom was God speaking when He said: "Let us?" According to the Holy Scriptures, as explained elsewhere in this presentation, He was talking to the Prince of the universe, The Messiah. In the first verse of the first chapter of Genesis, Moses uses words which indicate there is more than one person in the Godhead: "In the beginning God *['Elohim]* created the heaven and the earth." Genesis 1:1. The Hebrew word *'Elohim* ("Gods") is the plural form in Hebrew. Therefore, the verse could read: "In the beginning **Gods** [or the Godhead] created the heaven and the earth." The word "God" appears over 30 times in the first chapter of Genesis, and in Hebrew it is in the plural form, **'Elohim.**

The first chapter of Genesis also records what God created each day. Concerning the sixth day we read: "And God

['Elohim] said: Let Us make man in Our image, after Our likeness." Genesis 1:26. "And the LORD [YHWH] God ['Elohim] said: Behold, the man is become as one of us." In Genesis 11:6,7 it is recorded that: The Lord said, "Come, Let Us go down, and there confound their language." Again, we ask, who was the Lord addressing when He said, "Let Us"? **Rashi,** the noted Jewish commentator, suggests that God was addressing angels. Angels, however, were themselves created. Therefore, they cannot create. Furthermore, the Scripture declares that man was created "in the image of God." Genesis 1:27 . Nowhere, in Holy Writ, is man declared to have been created in the image of the angels.

It was evidently another Divine Being that God addressed when He said: "Let Us make man." But who was that other Divine being? He was none other than the Son of God, The Messiah. It does not take more than one God to rule the world. There is only one God the Father, but the very fact that He has with Him an associate seated at the right of His throne whom He calls His Anointed One or Messiah, and who is called the great Prince, means that this second person is a member of the royal household of the universe. Therefore, the word "God" is a generic term used to denote a Deity or Divine Being, and as such it can be applied to both the Lord God the Father and to His anointed Son The Messiah. When the Lord God the Father spake and said, "Let Us make man in Our image, after Our likeness" , He was addressing The Messiah.

Someone may say, What about the Shema? Isn't that translated at times, "Hear, O Israel, the Lord our God is one Lord?" Yes, that is the way it is translated in some Bibles, but that isn't the way it reads in the Hebrew Bible. To begin with, the word "LORD" is not at the end in that text. However, the name of God which is pronounced in Hebrew Yahveh, or Yahweh, does appear. Every pious Jew frequently recites the Shema:"Hear, O Israel: The Lord our God, the Lord is one." Deuteronomy 6:4. It should be noted that in Hebrew the above words "our God" are in reality "our Gods" ('**Eloheinu),** and the word meaning "God" is in the plural and not singular. Hence the more correct rendering of this text would be: "Hear, O Israel, the Lord our Gods ['**Elohim**] is one ['**echad**] Lord."

The Hebrew word 'echad denotes unity of a uniplural or a combined association of more than one member or party rather than a unity consisting of solely one individual member or party. Thus, for example, when God gave to Adam his wife

Eve, it was said of them: "And they shall be one [echad]
flesh." Genesis 2:24. In this scripture the two parties - man and
wife - are declared to be one [echad] - a unity. When God
made the first day of the week, the record says that it consisted
of two parts - evening and morning. Yet the Scripture says in
Genesis 1:5 (literally): "And-there-was evening and - there -
was morning: day one ['echad]" That is, the first day was a
unit consisting of two parts. Ezra 2:64 literally says of all the
people assembled: "All the congregation (was) as one [ki-
'echad] forty-two thousand three hundred (and) sixty."

When the Holy Scriptures speak of a unit consisting of only
one individual, to the exclusion of every other, it uses **yachid**.
Take, for instance, the case of Abraham when God bade him to
offer up his only son, Isaac: "Take now thy son, thine only
[yachid] son." Genesis 22:2. The Hebrew word yachid and
not 'echad is used here to designate a sole individual. The
Shema does not say, "Hear O Israel: The Lord our God is one
[yachid] Lord," as if the deity consists of solely one Divine
Person; but it says, "The Lord our God is one ['echad] Lord,"
as a uniplural or combined membership of Divine Persons.

CHAPTER 4

THE 490 YEAR PROPHECY

IN THESE days of increased knowledge, men and women are not interested in hearsay; they want facts. This applies particularly to the question of The Messiah. And concerning this, God has not left us in darkness. He has given us the necessary evidence as to the identity of The Messiah in His holy Word, the Bible, a great light which illuminates the future. This is made clear in Psalm 119:105, where we read: "Thy word is a lamp unto my feet, and a light unto my path." The reason why many men and women are living in gross darkness concerning the future of God's eternal plan is because they are not students of the Bible. It is unfortunate that the Scriptures are not being read and studied. The LORD has assured us that if we earnestly read and study His Word, He will reveal the future to us; its rays of light will shine upon our pathway that we may know where we are going. Regarding the days to come, God has declared:"Behold, the former things are come to pass, and new things do I declare; before they spring forth I tell you of them."Isaiah 42:9.The Hebrew Prophets declare: "Remember the former things of old: that I am God... and there is none like Me; declaring the end from the beginning, and from ancient times things that are not yet done." Isaiah 46:9, 10.

Our everlasting God knows all things, the future is equally present with Him. More so, perhaps, than any other one thing, the prophecies of the Bible and their fulfillment witness to its divine inspiration. Hence, man does not need to guess. He may know the future if he will diligently study the Holy Scriptures. We read regarding this: "For the LORD ETERNAL will do nothing unless He have revealed His secret unto His servants the prophets." Amos 3:7. If then, God does nothing unless He revealeth His secret unto His servants the prophets, we may believe that such an important event as the coming of The Messiah most certainly would be revealed. And this is what has been done. God has not only revealed the identity of The Messiah, *He has revealed the very year when The Messiah would come.* Think of it! the very year of The Messiah's appearing was foretold and Daniel was God's chosen servant through whom it was made known. Let us read in the Torah

these words of Moses: "The secret things belong unto the
LORD our God; but the things that are revealed belong unto us
and to our children forever." Deuteronomy 29:28. Consider
what God has revealed to us on this important matter. A
careful study of the very important prophecy of Daniel 9:24-27
reveals that there are two main events mentioned in connection
with Messiah's advent: (1) the restoration of the city of
Jerusalem, the Temple to be rebuilt, and the people of Israel to
return home from captivity in Babylon; (2) the destruction of
Jerusalem, the Temple to be destroyed, and the people of Israel
to be driven out of their country. We know that the people of
Israel were captive in Babylon for 70 years. They returned to
their homeland and rebuilt the city of Jerusalem and its
Temple. Their 70 year captivity had been foretold by the
Hebrew prophet Jeremiah, and the prophecy was accurately
fulfilled when the Jews returned to their homeland. In 70 C.E.,
Jerusalem and the Temple were destroyed by the Romans and
the people of Israel were driven from their homelands, to
become wanderers in all parts of the world.

Daniel's true prophecy of the coming of The Messiah is
found in that which is known as the prophetic period of the 70
weeks, or 490 years (Daniel 9:24-27). This period was to begin
with three events: The restoration of the people of Israel to
their homeland (verse 25), the rebuilding of Jersusalem (verse
25), and the rebuilding of the Temple (verse 25). The close of
the 490-year prophetic period is followed (in 70 C.E.) by three
events: The destruction of the Temple (verses 26, 27), the
destruction of Jerusalem (verse 26, 27), and the dispersion of
the Jews from their homeland (verses 26, 27). All of these
things took place, at the beginning and at the end of this
wonderful prophecy, as foretold. But what was to happen
during these 490 years? If the commencement of, and the
sequel to the prophecy were accurately fulfilled (and remember
it was written nearly 600 years before the events occurred) then
the prophecy of what was to happen during this period should
be accurately fulfilled also. As *Jewish people,* we must admit
we have waited several millenniums for the coming of The
Messiah and, so far as most of us are concerned, He has not
come. For this reason, a large number of our people have
given up all hope that He will come, and many have even lost
faith in their religion. Our Holy Bible not only contains
prophecy that foretold the year of The Messiah's coming, but
also gives the very name by which He is to be known.

Furthermore, it tells us how we may know whether or not He has come.

We read these words recorded by Moses: "The scepter shall not depart from Judah, nor a lawgiver from between his feet; until Shiloh come, and unto Him shall the gathering of the people be." Genesis 49:10. Concerning this prophetic statement, we read from the writings of ancient Hebrew sages: "The scepter(staff) shall not depart from Judah alludes to The Messiah, son of David,: etc." **Midrash Rabbah,** on Genesis, chapter 97, NV, volume 2, p. 906, Soncino Press. These statements make it clear that The Messiah would come before the kingdom of Judah was to be no more. The last monarch to rule over Israel was King Herod Agrippa I who died in 44 C.E. From that day to this we have never had a king who held the scepter over Judea. What does this mean to us as Jews? Could it be that The Messiah has come and we did not know it? Before we answer this question, let us read from the Jewish prayer book used on the *Day of Atonement*. Notice this statement carefully and then read it again: "Our righteous anointed (Messiah) is departed from us: horror hath seized us, and we have none to justify us. He hath borne the yoke of our iniquities, and our transgression, and is wounded because of our transgression. He beareth our sins on his shoulder, that he may find pardon for our iniquities. We shall be healed by his wound at the time that the Eternal will create him (The Messiah) as a new creature. O bring Him up from the circle of the earth. Raise Him up from Seir, to assemble us the second time on Mount Lebanon, by the hand of Yinnon."–**Mahsor, Prayer Book for the Day of Atonement** (translated by A. Th. Phillips), p. 239, Hebrew Publishing Co. Is not this a tacit recognition that He–The Messiah–has come once and He is to come again?

That "Yinnon" refers to The Messiah is clear from the Talmud: "What is his (The Messiah's) name?–The School of R. Shila said: His name is Shiloh, for it is written, until Shiloh come. The school of R. Yannai said: His name is Yinnon, for it is written, His name shall endure forever; e'er the sun was, his name is Yinnon."–**Sanhedrin** 98b, p. 667, Soncino Press.The same thought is emphasized in this statement: "Whence do we know concerning King Messiah? Because it is said, 'His name shall endure forever. Before the sun his name shall be continued (Yinnon)' (Ps. lxxii. 17). Why was his name called Yinnon?–For he will awaken those who sleep at Hebron

out of the dust of the earth, therefore is His name called
Yinnon, as it is said, 'Before the sun his name is Yinnon.'
(ibid.)"–**Pirke de Rabbi Eliezer,** Translated by G. Friedlander,
p. 233, Bloch Publishing Company.

Let us carefully study this 490-year prophecy in detail; it
should bring great joy to all our hearts. We read: "In the first
year of Darius the son of Ahasuerus, of the seed of the Medes,
which was made king over the realm of the Chaldeans; in the
first year of his reign I Daniel understood by books the number
of the years, where of the word of the LORD came to Jeremiah
the prophet (in Jeremiah 25:11, 12; 29:10), that He would
accomplish 70 years in the desolations of Jerusalem." Daniel
9:1,2. Daniel knew that the 70 years of the Babylonian
captivity of the Jews were about to end and thus he prayed to
God for the promised restoration to take place: "And I set my
face unto the LORD God, to seek by prayer and supplication,
and I prayed unto the LORD my God, and made my confession,
and said, O Lord, the great and dreadful God, keeping the
covenant and mercy to them that love Him, and to them that
keep His commandments; we have sinned, and have,
committed iniquity, and have done wickedly, and have
rebelled, even by departing from Thy precepts and from Thy
judgments: . . . And whiles I was speaking, and praying, and
confessing my sin and the sin of my people Israel, and
presenting my supplication before the LORD my God for the
holy mountain of my God; yea, whiles I was speaking in
prayer, even the man Gabriel, whom I had seen in the vision at
the beginning, being caused to fly swiftly touched me about the
time of the evening oblation." Daniel 3-5, 20, 21. How quickly
God responded to the supplication of His servant, for He sent
the angel Gabriel, to make known to Daniel what he and his
people needed to know. The prophet says: " And he (Gabriel)
informed me, and talked with me, and said, O Daniel, I am now
come forth to make thee wise with understanding. At the
beginning of thy supplications the commandment came forth,
and I am come to shew thee; for thou art greatly beloved:
therefore understand the matter, and consider the vision."
Daniel 9:22, 23.

The heavenly messenger said: "O Daniel, I am now come
forth to make thee wise with understanding. Therefore,
understand the matter, and consider the vision." This word
"understand" is repeated three times. There must be something
important about this prophecy for this word to be mentioned so

often. Since this prophecy is of such vital importance, we will quote from the Hebrew Bible, giving a literal English translation of it: "Seventy weeks have been cut off unto thy people and unto thy holy city for to finish the transgression, and to make an end of the sins, and to make atonement for iniquity, and to bring in everlasting righteousness, and to seal the vision and prophecy, and to anoint the most holy. Know thou and understand thou: From the going forth of a commandment to restore and to rebuild Jerusalem unto Prince Messiah (shall be) seven weeks and sixty-two weeks; shall be restored and shall be built a broad street and a moat, and in the distress of the times. And after the sixty-two weeks Messiah shall be cut off, and not for Himself; and the people of the prince who shall come shall destroy the city and the sanctuary, and the end of it (shall be) with a flood, and until the end of the war desolations are determined. And He shall confirm a covenant to many for one week; and in the middle of the week He shall cause the sacrifice and the oblation to cease; and on account of the widespread abominations He shall make desolate, and until the consummation, and that determined shall be poured out upon the desolate." Daniel 9:24-27

What does the expression "seventy weeks" mean? The Hebrew word correctly translated into English as "weeks" is **shabu'im** in Daniel 9:24. It denotes a unit of seven, and may refer to a period of either seven days or seven years. Which of the two is intended must be decided by the context usage. Here are some facts for consideration: In his commentary on Daniel 9:24, Dr. Judah B. Slotki says concerning the "seventy weeks" that they represent 490 years (7 x 70 = 490), and that this prophecy is "an allusion to the Messianic era." See his book **Daniel, Ezra, Nehemiah,** pp. 77-79, Soncino Press. Also: "The cryptic phraseology may have been suggested by the seven-year cycle of Lev. xxv. The expression 'week of years' occurs in the Mishnah (Sanh. v.1)."–**ibid.,** p. 77. Isaac Leeser noted Hebrew scholar and Bible translator, has said: "Ancient Jewish writers thought that the second Temple stood 420 years, which, with the 70 years of the Babylonian captivity, make 490."–**The Twenty-four Books of the Holy Scriptures,** sixth edition, p. 907, Bloch Publishing Company. The Talmudic tractate **Nazir** 32b, p. 118 of the Soncino Press carries an editorial footnote (No. 7) which refers to Daniel 9:24-27 and states: "This prophecy was uttered at the beginning of the 70 years captivity in Babylon. From the restoration of the second destruction is said to have been 420 years, making in all 490, i.e., 70 weeks of years." In the **Midrash Rabbah**, on Lamentations, Proems, p. 65 of the Soncino Press, Daniel 9:27 is quoted, and an editorial footnote (No. 6) comments that " 'one week' in Dan. ix means a week of years."

From the Jewish writings it is clear that our Hebrew sages understood that God had allotted to the Jewish people 70 weeks of years–a total of 490 years–in which to bring in everlasting righteousness. Note verse 25, where the word "understand" is used for the third time: "Know thou and understand thou: From the going forth of a commandment to restore and to rebuild Jerusalem unto Prince Messiah [shall be] seven weeks [of years] and 62 weeks [of years]." We need now to find out when the commandment, or decree, to restore and to rebuild Jerusalem was given. Once that is established, we can surely know when The Messiah was to appear. Let us read the very words of that decree: "Artaxerxes, king of kings, unto Ezra the priest, the scribe of the Law of the God of heaven, and so forth. And now I make a decree, that all they of the people of Israel, and their priests and the Levites, in my realm that are minded of the own free will to go with thee to Jerusalem, Blessed by the LORD, the God of our fathers, who hath put such a thing as this in the kings' heart, to beautify the house of the LORD which is in Jerusalem." Ezra 7:12, 13, 27. That decree issued by Artaxerxes I (Longimanus), king of Persia, was put into effect in 457 B.C.E. See Ezra 7:7-9; 8:31-33. It is true that some commentators have assigned other dates for it, but they have overlooked one important fact. Three Persian kings had a part in the restoration and rebuilding of Jerusalem after the Babylonian exile of the Jewish people, and this work was not completed until this decree by King Artaxerxes was put into effect. King Cyrus issued his decree in 537 B.C.E. (Ezra 1:1-4; 2 Chronicles 36:22,23); King Darius 1 (Hystaspes), about 518 B.C.E. (Ezra 6:1-12); and King Artaxerxes I (Longimanus), in 457 B.C.E. (Ezra 7:1-26). It took these three royal decrees to effectively constitute "a commandment to restore and to rebuild Jerusalem" in fulfillment of Daniel 9:24-27. This is very evident from the Biblical record: "They built and finished it, according to the commandment of the God of Israel and according to the decree of Cyrus, Darius, and Artaxerxes King of Persia." Ezra 6:14.

It took the three royal decrees to carry out the "commandment of the God of Israel," and the restoration of chart shown below. This will enable us to understand the matter much more clearly. Recognizing the starting point of this prophecy as the autumn of 457 B.C.E., let us read again: "Seventy weeks (of years) are determined upon thy people and upon thy holy city, to finish the transgression, and to make an end of sins, and to make reconciliation for iniquity, and to bring in everlasting righteousness, and to seal up the vision and prophecy, and to anoint the most holy." Daniel 9:24. These 70 weeks of years, then, were allotted to the Jewish people to finish their transgressions, to bring in everlasting righteousness, and to anoint the most holy.

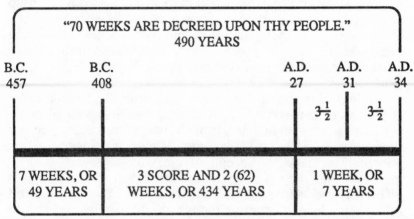

A chart of the "seventy weeks" which were decreed to God's people. Messiah's advent proved the prophecy true.

The 70 weeks of years are literally 490 years. Thus, 490 years were allotted to our people from the going forth of the final commandment in 457 B.C.E. to restore and rebuild Jerusalem. This became effective in the autumn of 457 B.C.E. It may readily be seen (see chart) that by adding the 490 years to that date we are brought to the autumn of 34 C.E., the end of the time period allotted for the Jewish people to make all things right between them and their God. Let us read again from Daniel: "Know thou and understand thou: From the going forth of a commandment to restore and to rebuild Jerusalem unto Prince Messiah (shall be) seven weeks (of years) and 62 weeks (of years)." Daniel 9:25.

Prince Messiah (shall be) seven weeks (of years) and 62 weeks (of years)." Daniel 9:25.

Before commenting further on this Biblical prophecy, it is interesting to note that many students are confronted with a serious problem concerning the various renderings of this text in the different English versions. Some of their versions punctuate the verse in one way and some in another. The punctuation greatly affects the interpretation. Thus, we must decide which is the correct punctuation in order to be assured as to its correct meaning. Punctuation marks in Bibles did not come into general use until the eighth century C.E. In the Hebrew Bibles these punctuation marks were added by a group of Hebrew Biblical scholars known as the Masoretes. They sought to put into the Written Word the traditional interpretation both of pronunciation and punctuation. These Masorete marks are still retained in the Hebrew Bibles used today.

An examination of the Hebrew in Daniel 9:25 reveals that at the end of the words "seven weeks" the Masoretes placed a punctuation stop, called an **athnach,** which corresponds to our semicolon. The fact that the Masoretes inserted this punctuation mark at the end of the words "seven weeks," indicates that they wanted to set the seven weeks off as a different and separate period from the 62-week period following. It may seem as though the Masoretes did this to confuse the Biblical student concerning the time prophecy of The Messiah's first coming. We may wonder why our Jewish spiritual leaders have not attempted to dispel the confusion created by our forefathers regarding this time prophecy.

For the benefit of those who may feel we are too drastic in this assertion, let us refer to a Talmudic passage undoubtedly written by a person who knew about this time prophecy, and who wrote these words forbidding our Jewish people to study it. We read: "R. Samuel b. Nahmani said in the name R. Jonathan: Blasted be the bones of those who calculate the end."–**Sanhedrin** 97b, volume 2, p. 659, Soncino Press. Editorial footnote No. 6 says: "i.e., Messiah's advent."

Returning to the question of punctuation marks, there is ancient evidence for placing the punctuation stop at the end of the words "sixty-two weeks," as do some English versions. For instance the Septuagint (which is the Hebrew Bible translated into Greek by 70 rabbis in the third century B.C.E.) gives in later editions, the punctuation marks. The Greek

Bibles are older than the Masoretic marks of the Hebrew Bibles. The Peshitta, the Syriac Bible written about the second century C.E., agrees with the Septuagint in placing the punctuation mark after the 62-week period, thus including the seven weeks to make the entire period amount to 69 weeks.

Generally speaking, the punctuation must be determined by the sense of the passage that accords with the intent of the writer and which harmonizes with other Biblical passages. Interpretations of those who deny the Messianic import of that passage overlook certain important factors of context and history. Conclusive evidence of the fact that the seven weeks and 62 weeks of Daniel 9:24 are to be considered a chronological unit of 69 weeks is implicit in the context (verses 24-27). The 70 weeks of Daniel 9:24-27 began in 457 B.C.E. At the time of the prayer and vision of chapter 9, Jerusalem lay desolate (verses 2, 11, 12, 16-19). In the answer to Daniel's prayer, the angel Gabriel assured him that the city would be rebuilt (verses 24, 25). This prediction was fulfilled in 45 B.C.E., when Artaxerxes I issued his decree for the complete restoration of the city (Ezra 5:13; 6:1, 14, 15; 7:8-28). The fate of Jerusalem and its Temple—the desolation and restoration—constitutes the theme of the chapter (Daniel 9:2, 16, 17, 19, 25-27). Soon after the close of the 70 weeks, Jerusalem was to be laid desolate again. This fact Daniel reiterates for emphasis and clarity (verses 26, 27). Yeshua specifically declared that the desolation thus predicted was still a future event in His day (Matthew 23:38; 24:3, 15-20; Mark 13:14; Luke 21:20-24).

As shown already from Jewish sources, these weeks in Daniel 9:24-27 are to be considered weeks of years, because history bears out the fact that Jerusalem and its Temple were not restored and rebuilt in seven literal weeks, nor in 62 literal weeks. Actually, it took approximately 49 literal years. If we were to accept the following rendering it would be even more confusing: "Know therefore and discern, that from the going forth of the word to restore and to build Jerusalem unto one anointed, a prince, shall be seven weeks; and for threescore and two weeks, it shall be built again, with broad place and moat, but in troublous time. By accepting the view set forth in authentic Jewish sources that the prophecy speaks of "weeks of years," and not weeks of days, we must conclude that this period of time would be 49 years, plus 434 years, making a total of 483 years. This would mean, according to the Jewish Bible from which we have just quoted, that The Messiah would have come at the end of the seven weeks or 49 years and would die or be cut off after 434 years! Notice how verse 26 reads in that version: "And after the threescore and two weeks shall an anointed one be cut off." Since threescore and two weeks equal 62 weeks of years, or 434 years, this would mean that The Messiah would have to have lived over 400 years and then be offered up as a sacrifice in order to become the Redeemer and Saviour of sinners! Thus, it can be seen that putting the punctuation mark in the wrong place makes the prophecy meaningless. This can only serve to hide the true meaning of the prophecy. To prove this, let us now read from Daniel 9:25 as it is correctly translated from the Hebrew, but ignoring the erroneous Masoretic punctuation mark: "Know thou and understand thou: From the going forth of a commandment to restore and to rebuild Jerusalem unto Prince Messiah (shall be) seven weeks and 62 weeks." The prophecy is simple and easy to understand, because seven weeks of years and 62 weeks of years gives us a total of 483 literal years from the going forth of the commandment to restore and build Jerusalem unto the time of The Messiah. It is well to note that this prophecy was fulfilled to the very year by Yeshua, The Messiah.

Referring to the chart again, add these 483 years to the time when the command went forth to restore and build Jerusalem, which was the autumn of 457 B.C.E. This brings us to 27 C.E., the very year appointed by God for The Messiah to make His public appearance. At the time appointed for all those entering the Jewish priesthood, 30 years of age, The Messiah appeared. His public appearance to commence His ministry began at the River Jordan, where John was immersing the repentant people in water by a rite that in some respects resembled that of Mikvah today. We read: "Then Yeshua comes from Galilee to John at the Jordan to be immersed by him. But he [John] forbade Him, saying: I have need to be immersed by Thee, and comest Thou to me? And answering, Yeshua said to him: Permit (it) now; for thus it becomes us to fulfill all righteousness. Then he permits Him. And having been immersed, Yeshua went up immediately from the water; and, lo, the heavens were opened, and he saw the Spirit of God descending as a dove, (and) coming upon Him. And, behold, a voice out of the heavens, saying: This is My beloved Son, in whom I have been well pleased." Matthew 3:13-17.

The Messiah appeared at the exact time God appointed for Him to begin His ministry, in the year 27 C.E. Let us read again from Daniel: "And after the 62 weeks (of years) Messiah shall be cut off, and not for Himself. . . . And He shall confirm a covenant for many for one week [of years]; and in the middle of the week He shall cause the sacrifice and the oblation to cease." Daniel 9:26, 27. From this we learn that The Messiah was to confirm the covenant for many for one more week of years, or seven years—the seventh and last of the 70 weeks allotted to the Jewish nation. Turning to the chart, you will notice that The Messiah appeared on time in 27 C.E.. Adding this one week of years, or seven years, to 27 C. E. brings us to 34 C.E., which marks the end of the 490-year period.

To recapitulate, first, we have found that God had allotted 490 years for the Jewish people to rebuild the city of Jerusalem and to make all things right. Then God said that from the going forth of the commandment to restore and rebuild Jerusalem unto The Messiah would be 483 years. Deducing the 483 years from the 490 years allotted to the Jewish people, we have exactly seven years, or one week of years remaining . This is the time referred to in the prophecy when The Messiah would confirm the covenant with many for one week of years or seven years. In the midst of the seven years, He would cause the sacrifice and oblation to cease. How? This is made plain in verse 26, it says: "Messiah shall be cut off, and not for Himself." Daniel 9:26. In other words, The Messiah was to be cut off or put to death, not for Himself but for the sins of the people. When was this to take place? In the midst of the seventh week of years. What is the midst of the middle of one week of years or seven years? three and one-half years. He taught the people, healed the sick, raised the dead, comforted the broken-hearted, and performed many other miracles during this period. He was much more than a mere man: He proved He was the Son of God, The Messiah, our Saviour and Redeemer.

At the end of His three and one-half years of ministry, the very time appointed by God, in the springtime (at the beginning of the Passover season) in 31 C.E., The Messiah was crucified by Roman soldiers. He was crucified at a place known in Hebrew as Golgotha [Calvary's Hill or place of the Skull]. This event was not a mere accident. Turning to the record, we marvel at the accuracy of this prophecy. The Messiah was crucified at the very time that the Passover lamb was slain as a sacrifice. An important aspect of this prophecy is the part concerning the restoration and destruction of Jerusalem and the

Temple, as recorded in these words: "Know thou and understand thou: From the going forth of a commandment to restore and to rebuild Jerusalem unto Prince Messiah [shall be] seven weeks [of years] and 62 weeks [of years]; shall be restored and shall be built a broad street and a moat, and in the distress of the times." Daniel 9:25. "The [Roman] people of the prince [Titus] who shall come shall destroy the city [Jerusalem] and the sanctuary [Temple], and the end of it [shall be] with a flood, and until the end of the war desolations [as a result] are determined. . . . And on account of the overspreading abomination he [Titus] shall make desolate, and until the consummation; and that determined [in the prophecy] shall be poured out upon the desolate." Daniel 9:26.

Our Jewish people were in captivity in Babylon for 70 years. During that time Daniel was informed in a message from God that they were to return to their homeland, to restore and to rebuild the city of Jerusalem. The final decree was issued for that purpose by King Artaxerxes I in 457 B.C.E. God says that after the restoration, The Messiah would come. Daniel 9:25 says: "Know thou and understand thou: From the going forth of a commandment to restore and rebuild Jerusalem unto Prince Messiah [shall be] seven weeks [of years] and 62 weeks [of years]." The divine pronouncement was that after The Messiah's coming, Jerusalem and its Temple would be destroyed by war:

The sacrificial system of ancient days pointed to The Messiah, who would come and die for our sins. All the sacrifices offered from the days of Adam down to the time of Moses and on, until the time of The Messiah pointed forward to the Lamb of God, who would come to die for our sins. In this act He would atone for both the guilt and penalty of sin. But notice that The Messiah died at the very time when the Passover lambs were slain in the Temple court. By His death He put an end, once and for all, to the sacrificial system. Concerning His crucifixion and death, we read: "And Yeshua, again crying out with a loud voice, yielded up His spirit. And, behold, the veil of the temple was rent in two from top to bottom, and the earth shook, and the rocks were split." Matthew 28:50,51.

Yeshua, The Messiah, was put to death on Friday afternoon, He lay in the tomb on the Sabbath, and on Sunday morning some of the women followers of The Messiah came to the tomb were He was buried. Concerning this, we read: "And answering, the angel said to the women: Fear ye not; for I know that ye seek Yeshua, the one having been crucified. He is not here, for He has been raised up, as He said. Come ye and see the place where He lay." Matthew 28:5, 6 . He [The Messiah] appeared to His disciples, and said: "Behold My hands and My feet, that it is I Myself: handle Me, and see; for a spirit hath not flesh and bones, as ye see Me have. And while they yet believed not for joy, and wondered, He said unto them, Have ye here any meat? And they gave Him a piece of a broiled fish, and of an honeycomb. And he took it, and did eat before them. And He said unto them, These are the words which I spake unto you, while I was yet with you, that all things must be fulfilled, which were written in the law of Moses, and in the prophets, and in the psalms, concerning Me. Then opened He their understanding, that they might understand the Scriptures." Luke 24:39-45.

The Messiah was crucified at the very time appointed by God and rose from the dead on the third day. Yeshua, undoubtedly, called the attention of the two disciples on the way to Emmaus to prophecies in the Hebrew Bible concerning His crucifixion. Among such prophecies were these: "The assembly of the wicked have enclosed Me; they pierced My hands and My feet." Psalms 22:17. "And they will look unto Me, whom they have pierced." Zechariah 12:10 . "And one shall say unto Him, What are these wounds in Thine hands? Then He shall answer, Those with which I was wounded in the house of My friends." Zechariah 13:6.

The Messiah was crucified three and one-half years after He began His ministry, or in the spring of 31 C.E. From this date until the end of the time allotted to the Jewish people, which was the autumn of 34 C.E., we have left exactly three and one-half years. This leaves three and one-half years from the time of the death and resurrection of The Messiah to the end of the time allotted to our forefathers. What event happened in the year 34 C.E? Many thousands of Jews accepted their Messiah during the three and one-half years that remained. History records that as many as 3,000 in one day accepted Yeshua, the Jewish Messiah. The number of men soon swelled to 5,000, and a great company of the priests were obedient to the faith. The majority of the Jewish people, however , did not. Instead of accepting Yeshua as The Messiah, they began to persecute those who did accept Him and drove them out of the country. But as the faithful were scattered into various countries, they carried with them the message of the true Messiah. In this way many people of the nations accepted the Jewish Messiah.

Let our minds remain clear as we consider this great prophecy that God gave to the Hebrew prophet Daniel concerning The Messiah. In this accurate prophecy, God outlined the history of Israel for 490 years and revealed that during this period The Messiah was to come. This time prophecy is so cogent and indisputable that we must honestly admit that either The Messiah has come or that He never will come. If the latter, then we shall have to conclude the Bible has failed, and all proof that there is a God who fulfills His Word is nonexistent. But let us not be deceived. There is an all-loving God who rules in the heavens above; and His Word, the Bible, has never failed in fulfilling one prophecy, and it never will fail. Remember, the beginning and ending of this 490-year prophecy is accurate as seen in the restoration and dispersion of Israel. Therefore, we must, of necessity and in all honesty, admit that the rest of the prophecy concerning The Messiah is also true. But we as a people failed to recognize and accept Him as our own Jewish Messiah. Think of it; this is exactly what God said would happen. Note these words recorded by the Hebrew prophet Isaiah: "He [The Messiah] was despised and rejected of men; a man of sorrows, and acquainted with grief: and as one from whom men hide their face He was despised and we esteemed Him not." Isaiah 53:3. "All we like sheep, have gone astray; we have turned every one to his own way; and the LORD hath caused the iniquity of us all to fall upon Him [The Messiah]." Verse 6. "He [The Messiah] was oppressed, and He was afflicted, yet He opened not His mouth: as a lamb which is brought to the slaughter, and as a sheep before her shearers is dumb, so He opened not His mouth." Verse 7. "He [The Messiah] was wounded because of our transgressions, He was crushed because of our iniquities. . . . The LORD hath made to light on Him the iniquity of us all. . . . He was cut off out of the land of the living, for the transgression of my people to whom the stroke was due." Isaiah 53:5, 6, 8.

We read from our Jewish Prayer Book what we have just read from the Holy Bible: "May it be Thy will that the sounds of the Shofar (Ram's Horn) which we have sounded today be woven into Thy tapestry Yeshua, the Prince of Thy presence and Prince of might. So mayest Thou receive our pleas and extend to us Thy compassion." **Prayer Book for the New Year.**—Translated by Dr. A. Th. Phillips, revised and enlarged, p. 100, Hebrew Publishing Company. "Our righteous anointed [Messiah] is departed from us: horror hath seized us, and we have none to justify us. He hath borne the yoke of our iniquities, and our transgression, and is wounded because of our transgression. He beareth our sins on His shoulder, that He may find pardon for our iniquities. We shall be healed by His wound, at the time that the Eternal will create Him [The Messiah] as a new creature. O bring Him up from the circle of the earth. Raise Him up from Seir, to assemble us the second time on Mount Lebanon, by the hand of Yinnon."–**Prayer Book for the Day of Atonement,** as translated by Dr. A. Th. Phillips, p. 239, Bloch Publishing Company.

To attempt to deny the above prophecy would be dishonest to ourselves and to God, who desires to save us for eternity through our own Messiah. His first coming was for the purpose of atoning for our guilt by paying the penalty for our sins, so that we may receive pardon by accepting Him who never sinned, but died for our sins. This is the purpose of God in the work of The Messiah: He is our Redeemer, our Saviour. Sin is the transgression of the law, and the wages of sin condemned man to eternal death. Therefore God provided a substitute in the person of the Prince of the Universe, Yeshua The Messiah.

After reading the above quotations from the prayer book, one might ask, Did the Hebrew sages of old know all this concerning The Messiah when they wrote the prayer books? The answer is obvious. *They must have known!* The sages who wrote the prayer found on page 239 in the **Prayer Book for the Day of Atonement** have quoted several parts of one of the Messianic chapters of the Hebrew Bible. Let us read and see that they took their words and thoughts for this prayer as follows: "(3) He (is) despised and forsaken of men, a man of sufferings and acquainted with grief; and as one from whom men hide their faces he has been despised, and we have not esteemed him. (4) Surely our infirmities he has borne, and carried our sufferings; and we deemed him one stricken, smitten of God, and afflicted. (5) And he (was) wounded on account of our transgressions, he was bruised on account of our iniquities; the chastisement of our peace (was) upon him, and by means of his stripes we have been healed. (6) All of us have gone astray as sheep; each one to his own way, we have turned away our faces; and the LORD has caused the iniquity of all of us to fall on him. (7) He was oppressed, and was afflicted, and he opened not his mouth: he (was) brought as the lamb to the slaughter, and dumb as a sheep before its shearers, he opened not his mouth. (8) From prison and from judgment he was taken; and his generation, who shall tell of it? Because he has been cut off from the land of the living, on account of the transgression of my people he has been stricken to death. (9) And he made his grave with the wicked, and with a rich man in his death; because no violence has he done, and no deceit (was) in his mouth. (10) And the LORD was pleased to bruise him; He caused (him) grief, if he should set forth his soul a guilt-offering; he shall see seed, he shall prolong (his) days, and the pleasure of the LORD shall prosper by his hand. (11) The travail of his soul he shall see; he shall be satisfied; by his knowledge My righteous servant shall bring righteousness to many, and their iniquities he shall bear. (12) For this reason I shall divide (a portion) to him with many, and with mighty ones he shall divide a spoil, because that he has poured out his soul unto the death, and with transgressors he was numbered, and he bore the iniquity of many, and for the transgressors he shall intercede." Isaiah 53:3-12.

Additionally, one may ask how the sages who wrote the Prayer Book knew that the name of The Messiah was Yeshua, as quoted above in the Mahsor for the New Year? The answer is that they understood what the Bible teaches concerning The Messiah. There are a few places in the Hebrew Bible where The Messiah is referred to as Yeshua. Note the word "salvation" underlined in this text: "Behold, the LORD has proclaimed unto the end of the earth: say ye to the daughter of Zion: 'Behold, thy salvation cometh; behold, His reward is with Him, and His recompense before Him.' And they shall call them Thy holy people, The redeemed of the LORD." Isaiah 62:11, 12. In that passage the Hebrew word rendered as "salvation" is yesha', and it is so translated in most instances. As such it refers to a phase of religion, a principle or benefit which the individual receives from God. At times, however, the thought is that of a person, and in some of the Hebrew writings, we find this mentioned. In Isaiah 12:2 we read: "Behold, God is my salvation (**yeshu'ah**)." The **Midrash Rabbah,** on Exodus, chap. 23, section 6, in quoting Psalm 19:17 says: "I will sing of Thy strength, refers to the Messianic era, for it says, <u>Behold, God is my salvation; I will trust, and not be afraid</u> (Isa. xii. 2)."–page 284, Soncino Press.

In the Hebrew text of Zechariah 9:9, the prophet says: "Behold, thy king shall come to thee, just and having salvation (**nosha'**)." As anciently rendered into Greek by Hebrew scholars, it says: "Behold, thy king is coming to thee, just and a saviour (Gr., **sozon,** 'one saving')," etc. See the Septuagint (LXX) text. However, Dr. A. Cohen's commentary on Zechariah 9:9 says: "Thy king cometh unto thee. This can only refer to King Messiah, of whom it is said, And his dominion shall be from sea to sea," etc.–**The Twelve Prophets,** p. 305, Soncino Press. Thus the "Saviour" of Zechariah 9:9, is equated with The Messiah, or Yeshua. The one sent to save us, as set forth in both Isaiah 12:2 and Zechariah 9:9, is The Messiah, who brings us salvation as stated in Isaiah 62:11, 12.

Someone may ask, Why did the Hebrew sages write in the **Prayer Book, New Year,** p. 100, the prayer to God, "May He appear the second time?" Evidently because He came once, which most of the Jewish people do not believe. Let us ever remember that among the Hebrew sages were many honest men who knew and wrote truth. On the other hand, there were Hebrew sages that were not so honest. Note two quotations particularly, the first one of an honest-hearted sage who wrote: "May He appear the second time." The men who wrote this could have known of the prophecy of the 490 years, and thus they knew He had to come during the time of the second Temple, which is between the beginning and ending of this 490-year prophecy. That some did know is evident form the following Talmudic statement: "The Tanna debe Eliyyahu taught: The world is to exist 6,000 years; the first 2,000 years are to be void; the next 2,000 years are the period of the Torah, and the following 2,000 years are the period of the Messiah."– 'Abodah Zarah 9a, p. 43, Soncino Press. It appears that some of the Hebrew scholars who wrote the Talmud knew that The Messiah would come after about 4,000 years of earth's history. Therefore, it is no marvel if they wrote in the prayer book what they already knew from the teaching of the Bible and Talmud. Though they wrote honestly, because of prevalent prejudice, they may not have known the true identity of the Jewish Messiah.

The question may be asked by some of our Jewish people, "If The Messiah has already come the first time, as has been shown in this study, why don't our rabbis know about this?"

One of our rabbis who wrote a portion of the Talmud evidently knew about this prophecy, for he forbade anyone to study the book of Daniel concerning the prophetic time period. Notice these statements taken from the Talmud: "The Targum of the Pentateuch was composed by Onkelos the proselyte. . . . The Targum of the Prophets was composed by Jonathan ben Uzziel . . . and a Bath Kol came forth and exclaimed, Who is this that has revealed My secrets to mankind? Jonathan b. Uzziel thereupon arose and said, It is I who have revealed Thy secrets to mankind. It is fully known to Thee that I have not done this for my own honor, . . . He further sought to reveal by a targum [the inner meaning] of the Hagiographa, but a Bath Kol went forth and said, Enough! What was the reason?–Because the date of the Messiah is foretold in it."–**Megillah** 3a, pp. 9, 10, Soncino Press. Footnote 2 on p. 10 says: "The reference is probably to the Book of Daniel." "R. Samuel b. Nahmani said in the name of R. Jonathan: Blasted be the bones of those who calculate the end."–**Sanhedrin** 97b, volume 2, p. 659, Soncino Press. Footnote 6, "i.e, Messiah's advent." Footnote 4, "The verses cited from Daniel, the Psalms, and Haggai were interpreted so as to give a definite date for the advent of the Messiah."

Among our rabbis today are many pious men, yet they do not study the prophecies of the Bible and so do not know the truth concerning The Messiah. Nevertheless, a few rabbis who have studied the Messianic prophecies have accepted Yeshua as the one and only Jewish Messiah. The time is soon coming when many Rabbis and thousands of our Jewish people will join this great reformation among true Israelites.

Some of our Jewish people have the erroneous idea that if a Jew accepts Yeshua as The Messiah, he is no longer a Jew. This is not true! According to the Holy Scriptures, one does not fully know the joy of being a real Jew until he accepts Yeshua, The Messiah, and follows all the teachings of the Holy Scriptures. He knows what it means to be a real Jew when, by divine help, he keeps all the Ten Commandments. This includes the observance of the Sabbath from sunset Friday to sunset Saturday. He also refrains from eating trafe (unclean food), such as swine's flesh and fish without fins and scales, which Moses recorded in the Torah as being condemned by God.

It has been said that if The Messiah had come, we would now have a utopia on earth. However, according to the Holy

Bible, when the plan of salvation is thoroughly studied and rightly understood, we find that The Messiah has to come twice. At His first coming He was to suffer by taking our guilt and paying the penalty for our sins. The Messiah committed no sin, yet was tempted in all points as we are, but He did not yield to sin. Therefore, He is our Saviour and Redeemer. So all who accept Him as their Saviour and Redeemer need not die for their sins, because by accepting Him as their personal Saviour, the death penalty for them has been paid. However, remember that the sinner who willfully rejects The Messiah as his personal Saviour will have to meet the penalty for his own iniquities and will die an eternal death.

The Messiah's second coming, however, is altogether different. His purpose will be to reward all people. The righteous, and the ungodly. All the righteous and pious people will be delivered from evil and redeemed for eternity, and they will live in utopia forever; but all sinners will be destroyed. Therefore, it is for us to make the decision. Are we going to accept the testimony of the Holy Scriptures, the Bible, as God gave them to us, or are we going to forsake them as many have done? It must be remembered that had our forefathers diligently studied the Holy Scriptures instead of following the traditions of men, many would have accepted The Messiah. But, because they were following tradition, and not the teachings of the Holy Scriptures, many Jewish people in following their example have also forsaken their own Jewish Messiah. May God help us so to live and so to order our lives that we might be found among the holy and righteous who have accepted The Messiah as their personal Saviour. Thus we shall be ready when He comes the second time. Then as His children we shall live throughout eternity.

CHAPTER 5

God's Suffering Servant

IN CONSIDERING the vital subject, " God's," Suffering Servant," let us first refer to the Babylonian Talmud: "Rab said, The world was created only on David's account. Samuel said: On Moses' account; R. Johanan said: For the sake of the Messiah. What is his [The Messiah's] name?–The School of R. Shila said: His name is Shiloh, for it is written, <u>until Shiloh come</u>. . . . The Rabbis said: His name is 'the leper scholar,' as it is written, <u>Surely he hath borne our griefs, and carried our sorrows: yet we did esteem him a leper, smitten of God, and afflicted</u> [Isa. LIII, 4]."–**Sanhedrin** 98b, volume 2, pp. 667, 668, Soncino Press.

We find that our sages, many centuries ago, applied Isaiah 53 to The Messiah. Inasmuch as our forefathers, writing in the Talmud, applied Isaiah 53 to The Messiah, it is quite important for us to read the chapter and see just why they applied it to the Redeemer. The Bible as originally written was not separated into chapters. The divisions that we now have are basically man's conception of where the chapters should be divided, according to decisions reached by scholars for purposes of reference. However, as we read the Bible, we find that the division of chapter 53 was made just three verses too late. It obviously should be divided at chapter 52, verse 13, as one can see by a careful reading of the passage. The first part of the verse Isaiah 52:13 reads as follows: "Behold, My Servant shall prosper." Then in chapter 53, the last part of verse 11, we read "My Servant shall justify the righteous before many." Clearly this whole portion from Isaiah 52:13 to the end of Isaiah 53 deals with the Servant of God. The statement is corroborated by **The Jewish Encyclopedia** that states: "There are, however, four passages in the Isaiah compilation where perhaps the 'national' interpretation is not admissible, namely, Isa. xlii. 1-4, xlix. 1-6, I. 4-9, lii. 13-liii. 12. The description in them of the attitude and conduct of the 'ebed YHWH seem to be idealizations of the character of an individual rather than of the whole of Israel. Especially is this true of Isa. Iii. 13-Iiii. 12, the exaltation of the 'man of suffering'." volume 2, p. 204, article **"Servant of God."**

The topic chosen for this study is entitled "The Suffering Servant of God" because God Himself calls Him His Servant. In order that we may know who this Servant is and why our sages applied the title "Servant of God" to The Messiah, we will read from verse 13 of chapter 52 thru the first two verses of chapter 53. "Behold, My servant shall prosper, he shall be exalted and extolled, and be very high.   As many were astonished at Thee; his visage was so marred more than any man, and his form more than the sons of men: so shall he sprinkle many nations; the kings shall shut their mouths at him: for that which had not been told them shall they see; and that which they had not heard shall they consider. Who would have believed our report? and to whom is the arm of the LORD revealed? For he grew up before Him as a tender plant, and as a root out of a dry ground." Isaiah 52:13-53:2.

We find that God calls His Messiah "My Servant"; and of Him He said, "My Servant shall prosper. He shall be exalted and extolled, and be very high." Notice the prophet's description of this Servant in verse 14: "As many were astonished at Thee." Note the Bible answer. "His visage [appearance] was so marred more than any man, and his form more than the sons of men." That means exactly what it says. The work of The Messiah, in carrying out the plan of salvation to redeem man from sin, would be of such a nature as to mar His appearance and form (or the physical body). Verse 15 of Isaiah 52 indicates the relationship of The Messiah to other rulers. "So shall he startle many nations. Kings shall shut their mouths because of him." Here we see that The Messiah's influence would be so great that "the kings of the earth shut their mouths at him." In other words, they, too, would pay respect to The Messiah, and it is indeed so. Today we find kings of the earth paying respect to The Messiah.

The first verse of Isaiah 53 reveals the way The Messiah would be received. "Who would have believed our report?" God, through the Hebrew prophet Isaiah, is speaking to His own Hebrew people, and in speaking of them, He asks, "Who would have believed our report?" Consider our Jewish people scattered over the world today. How many believe in The Messiah? Since God knew that our Jewish people as a nation would ignore or reject this report, He asks this question: "Who would have believed our report? and to whom is the arm of the LORD revealed?" In other words: To whom is revealed the plan of salvation through The Messiah? Who believes it?

Surely, with such words as these written in the Hebrew Bible, it is time that our Jewish people reconsider their position on The Messiah, and that they re-read these prophecies and find out to whom they apply.

As we continue to read Isaiah, chapter 53, we find the wording in this chapter of the Hebrew Bible, commonly called the Old Testament, sounds much like that in the New Testament. Verse 2: "For he grew up before Him as a tender plant, and as a root out of a dry ground: he had no form nor comeliness; and when we see him, there is no beauty that we should desire him." Why? The answer is found in chapter 52, verse 14: "As many were astonished at Thee; his visage was so marred more than any man, and his form more than the sons of men." Notice verse 3; God says concerning The Messiah: "He was despised and rejected of men; a man of sorrows, and acquainted with grief: and we hid as it were our faces from him; he was despised, and we esteemed him not." Listen to the sad pronouncement: "He was despised, and we esteemed him not." We—who are we? *We, the Hebrew nation; we, the Jewish people.* We despised and rejected him. He is "a man of sorrows, and acquainted with grief: and we hid as it were our faces from him; he was despised, and we esteemed him not." How sad it is that the majority of our Jewish people, our Hebrew nation, rejected and despised our own Jewish Messiah; and many in the gentile world accepted Him. Today the Jewish Bible is read and revered by millions in the Gentile world, the very Bible that so many of our Jewish people today seldom, if ever, read. Note verses 4 and 5: "Surely he hath borne griefs inflicted by us, and suffered sorrows we have caused: yet we did esteem him stricken, smitten of God, and afflicted. But he was wounded through our transgressions, bruised through our iniquities: the chastisement of our peace was upon him, and with his wounds we were healed."

The Bible teaches that sin is the transgression of the law of God, and that the wages of sin is death. Ezekiel 18:4, 20. Because we are all sinners, and all have failed and come short of the glory of God, we are all doomed to eternal death. That is why we need The Messiah to redeem us from the penalty of sin. How could this be done? Only by The Messiah himself paying the penalty for our sins. Thus by dying for our sins and then rising from the grave, He is now our Redeemer. When we accept The Messiah as our Redeemer, His death stands in our behalf, so that we do not have to die for our sins. When we accept The Messiah as our Saviour Redeemer, His death becomes the propitiation for our sins. Let us notice these tender words: "He hath borne griefs inflicted by us. . . . He was wounded through our transgressions." Our eternal life and eternal peace depended upon Him. He had to resist sin and eventually die to pay the penalty for our sin: thus our peace and our eternal life depended upon implementing God's plan of salvation for us. Verse 6 aptly describes our condition: "All we like sheep have gone astray we have turned every one to his own way; and the LORD hath caused the iniquity of us all to fall upon him [The Messiah]."

We, the sons and daughters of Abraham, for almost 2,000 years have gone astray; we have strayed from our own Jewish Messiah. "He was oppressed, and he was afflicted, yet he opened not his mouth: as a lamb which is brought to the slaughter, and as a sheep before her shearers is dumb, so he opened not his mouth." Let us consider the foregoing passage. "He was oppressed, and he was afflicted, yet He opened not his mouth." He was taken as a prisoner. He was beaten first at the trial of the Sanhedrin. Next he was taken before Pilate, and then before King Herod. After this, He was sent back to be tried again before Pilate, who sentenced Him to die on a pagan cross. Roman soldiers took Him and nailed Him to it. Thus it was fulfilled, as Isaiah had said: "He was oppressed, and he was afflicted, yet he opened not his mouth: as a lamb which is brought to the slaughter." The New Testament says that when John the Immerser saw The Messiah by the River Jordan, he said, "Behold the Lamb of God, which taketh away the sin of the world." John 1:29. John, a Hebrew of the priestly order, recognized our Messiah as the Lamb of God that would take away the sin of the world.

Isaiah 53, verse 8 reads: "By oppression and judgment he was taken away, and with his generation who did reason? For he was cut off out of the land of the living." "Cut off out of the land of the living" means that he was put to death. A similar statement is found in Daniel 9:26: "And after threescore and two weeks shall the anointed [Messiah] be cut off." He died for us, that we might live and have eternal life. Why was He to be put to death? Notice the last part of Isaiah 53:8: "For the transgression of My people." He was put to death, for the sins of the Hebrew people and for those of all other members of the human family who would accept Him as The Messiah. These Bible texts are echoed in the New Testament. But we are reading a portion of Isaiah's prophecy written nearly 800 years before The Messiah came to this world. Verse 9 tells of what would befall The Messiah at the time of his death.

In order to get a correct view of the teaching of Isaiah 52:13 to 53:12, it is necessary to note particularly the pronouns used in reference to the parties mentioned in this passage from Holy Writ. We will list them as follows:

He is despised .... v. 3
He is a man of sorrows .... v. 3
He hath borne our griefs .... v. 4
He is smitten.. v. 4
He was wounded .... v. 5
He was bruised .... v. 5
He was oppressed .... v. 7
He was cut off .... v. 8
He did no violence .... v. 9
He made His grave with the wicked .... v. 9

Several verses speak of "His" and "Him."

We like sheep have gone astray .... v. 6
We have turned ... to our own way .... v. 6
We esteemed Him not .... v. 3
We hid our faces .... v. 4
We did esteem Him stricken .... v. 4
We did esteem Him smitten .... v. 4
We did esteem Him afflicted .... v. 4
We are healed by His stripes.......................... v. 5
We did not desire Him .... v. 2
We were like sheep .... v. 6

Such words as "us" and "our" also are used several times.

The question naturally arises, to whom do the "He" texts refer? To whom are the "We" texts to be applied? The "He" did something for "us." "We" did something for "him."

For an answer to our query, let us notice the translation of Isaiah 53 as presented by some of our much-respected teachers. For example, the great Jewish scholar Ibn Ezbra (1070 - after 1138 C.E.), who "was an unrivaled master of the Hebrew language" (**The Jewish Encyclopedia,** vol. 6, p. 525), has left behind his commentary on Isaiah, from which we quote his rendering of Isaiah 53:4-6, as translated into English by Dr. Michael Friedlander: "Surely he hath borne the griefs, and suffered the sorrows caused by us: yet we did esteem him stricken, smitten of God, and afflicted. But he was wounded by our transgressions, he was bruised by our iniquities: a chastisement which caused our peace was upon him; and with his stripes we were healed. All we like sheep have gone astray; we have turned every one to his own way; and the LORD hath laid on him the punishment we all deserved."–**The Commentary of Ibn Ezbra on Isaiah,** volume 2, p. 87, Society of Hebrew Literature.

In a penitential prayer recited on **Yom Kippor** sentiments very similar to those of Isaiah 53 are expressed: "We have trespassed, we have dealt treacherously, we have robbed, we have spoken slander, we have acted perversely and we have wrought wickedness, we have acted presumptuously, we have done violence, we have framed lies, we have counselled evil, we have spoken falsely, we have scoffed, we have revolted, we have provoked, we have rebeled, we have committed iniquity, we have transgressed, we have oppressed, we have been stiff-necked, we have acted wickedly, we have corrupted, we have committed abomination, we have gone astray, we have led [others] astray."–**Prayer Book for the Day of Atonement,** edited by A. Th. Phillips, revised addition, p.129 Hebrew Publishing Company.

The language is very similar to that used in the verses quoted above from Isaiah's prophecy. This means, then, that the "We" texts apply to us. We have done something to "Him." But who is the servant referred to as "He" or "Him"? Again, why not let our ancient fathers tell us? They may prove to be reliable guides in this matter.

A careful study of the ancient interpretations reveals the fact that the Messianic application of Isaiah 53 was quite generally acknowledged by our early teachers until about 1150 C.E. An excellent compilation of these testimonies was made some years ago, and the following statements are from this compilation.

As stated in the beginning of this book in a discussion of the Talmudic Sages concerning the names by which The Messiah would by called: "The Rabbis said: His name is 'the leper scholar,' as it is written, <u>Surely he hath borne our griefs, and carried our sorrows: yet we did esteem him a leper, smitten of God, and afflicted</u> [Isa. LIII, 4]."–**Sanhedrin** 98b volume 2,

p. 668, Soncino Press. The **Midrash Rabbah**, on Ruth, chapter 6, section 6, in comment on Ruth 2:14 says: "The fifth interpretation makes it refer to the Messiah. COME HITHER: approach to royal state. AND EAT OF THE BREAD refers to the bread of royalty; AND DIP THY MORSEL IN THE VINEGAR refers to his sufferings, as it is said, BUT HE WAS WOUNDED BECAUSE OF OUR TRANSGRESSIONS' (Isa. LIII, 5)."–Soncino Press.

Now let us note again Isaiah 53:9: "And they made his grave with the wicked, and with the rich his tomb; although he had done no violence, neither was any deceit in His mouth." Note the fulfillment of this prophecy as recorded in Matthew 27:38: "Then were there two thieves crucified with Him, one on the right and another on the left." He was put to death as if He were a criminal, but was "with the rich in His tomb." How was He with the rich? Let us read in the record: "There came a rich man from Arimathea named Joseph, . . . approaching Pilate the same man asked for the body of Yeshua. . . And taking the body, Joseph wrapped it (in) a clean sheet and placed it in his new tomb which he had hewed in the rock." Matthew 27:57-60. In His death The Messiah was laid in a rich man's tomb, This is the fulfillment of Isaiah's prophecy concerning The Messiah's death and burial.

Isaiah 53:10, 11 reads; "And the LORD was pleased to bruise him; He caused [Him] grief, if he should set forth his soul a guilt-offering; and he shall prolong [His] days, and the pleasure of the LORD shall prosper by his hand, and he shall see a seed, he shall be satisfied; by his knowledge My righteous servant shall bring righteousness to many, and their iniquities he shall bear."

God says that He would be pleased when The Messiah would make his soul an offering for sin. Why? Because God's love is so great . The Bible says, "For God so loved the world, that He gave His only begotten Son, that whosoever believeth in Him should not perish, but have everlasting life." John 3:16. He so loved us that He wanted us to have eternal life, and all who accept His Messiah as their Redeemer will receive eternal life. Thus it pleased the God of Israel when The Messiah made His soul an offering for sin. Isaiah 53 could not apply to any ordinary man. It is speaking only of the "Suffering Servant of God," the One who would be born into this world and would grow up as a child, as a plant out of a dry ground.

The next portion of Isaiah 53:10 says, "He shall see his seed, he shall prolong his days." After He had made His soul an offering for sin, He then is able to see His seed. Notice the significance of this statement. It means that He would live again; "He shall see his seed," His followers, the righteous who are saved through His redemption for us, "He shall prolong his days, and the pleasure of the LORD shall prosper in his hand." Verse 10.

Isaiah 53:11 reveals The Messiah's attitude toward His own sacrifice. "He shall see of the travail of His soul, and shall be satisfied." And it adds: "By His knowledge My righteous Servant shall bring righteousness to many." Verse 11. Why? The explanation given is that "He shall bear their iniquities." The Messiah bore our iniquities when He died on Calvary's cross. Remember this! we must accept Him as our personal Saviour and get ready for His soon coming. For The Messiah will come very soon–in this generation. We are now living in the latter days of this earth's history–we are living in the Messianic days just before the coming of The Messiah. We must get ready to meet Him. Remember that God wants us to keep all of His commandments, including the Seventh day Sabbath, we are not to eat anything that is trafe [unclean]. We must become real Jews, true Believers in The Messiah, who follow the religion of our God, the religion of the Bible. Therefore, let us be faithful Jews. In God's sight, he is not a Jew who is merely one outwardly, but he is a Jew who is one inwardly.

Many of our Jewish people today, sad to say, are not Jews at heart. Spiritually they are no better than the unbelieving goyim [Gentiles], because they do not keep the Sabbath, they do not observe the clean and unclean laws of Moses, and they do not accept The Messiah. They are disobedient and without hope in this world. Note: Isaiah 53:12. "Therefore will I divide him a portion among the great, and he shall divide the spoil with the mighty; because he bared his soul unto death, and was numbered with the transgressors; yet he bore the sin of many, and made intercession for the transgressors."

The record says: He was crucified and put to death with two thieves. He was not considered a righteous man. He was condemned as a transgressor by most of His own Jewish people. We read in the final part of the text, "He [The Messiah] bore the sins of many." Verse 12. This includes all who accept Him as their personal Saviour. "And made intercession for the transgressors." The question may arise, interceded before whom? The answer is—before God. God, the Ancient of days, sits as the Judge, and we are condemned as sinners, but The Messiah intercedes for us. As if He were our attorney, He pleads our case before the God of Heaven, the Father of the universe. He says: My Father, my blood was shed for these who have accepted Me as their personal Saviour and Redeemer, I intercede and plead for them that they might have eternal life.

This list of facts from Isaiah 53 pictures clearly the nature and work of the Servant of the Lord. Note that it portrays The Messiah as:

A human personality .... v.
An innocent sufferer.............................. vv. 9, 12
A voluntary sufferer .... vv. 4, 11
A silent sufferer .... v. 7
A vicarious sufferer .... v. 10
A substitutionary sufferer .... vv 6, 8,10,11,12
A sufferer who dies .... vv. 8, 10, 12
A redemptive sufferer .... v. 5
A sufferer who is resurrected .... v. 11

These Biblical expressions were also applied by our ancient fathers as refering to a righteous Messiah who has suffered for us. In our own Prayer Book reference is made to The Messiah in relation to Isaiah 53 as follows: "Our righteous anointed [**Mashiach,** Messiah] is departed from us: horror hath seized us, and we have none to justify us. He hath borne the yoke of our iniquities, and our transgressions, and is wounded because of our transgression. He beareth our sins on his shoulder, that he may find pardon for our iniquities. We shall be healed by his wound, at the time that the Eternal will create him [The Messiah] as a new creature. O bring him up from the circle of the earth. Raise him up from Seir, to assemble us the second time on Mount Lebanon, by the hand of Yinnon."–**Prayer Book for the Day of Atonement,** edited by Dr. A. Th. Phillips, revised and enlarged, p. 239, Hebrew Publishing Company. Think of it! He would go to the grave, but He would not be left there. He would be placed in the tomb, but He would not see corruption [decay]. This is a remarkable statement. Those placed in the grave go to corruption, so obviously He must be raised from the dead. This is what happened. He came forth from the tomb on the third day.

It is interesting to note that concerning The Messiah, as foretold in Psalm 16:9, 10, our ancient leaders taught: "<u>Therefore my heart is glad</u> (Ps. 16:9), glad in the words of the Torah; and my glory in the Lord Messiah who will rise up out of me. Of this it is written <u>And over all the glory be a canopy</u> (Isa. 4. 5)." "<u>My flesh also dwelleth in safety</u> (Ps. 16. 9)– dwells in safety even after death. R. Isaac said: This verse proves that neither corruption nor worms had power over David's flesh."–**Midrash on Psalms,** on Psalm 16, volume. 1, p. 201, Yale University Press. Note the six words, "dwells in safety even after death."

By His death, our sinless Messiah paid the death penalty that we deserve. God had a purpose in sending us His Messiah. He would be the vicarious sacrifice for the sins of men; He would bear their guilt to the grave. He would rise from the dead and sit at the right hand of God. There He ministers as our great High Priest in the Temple in heaven, fulfilling the prophecy in which God had said: "Thou art a priest for ever after the order of Melchizedek." Psalm 110:4. Also: "He shall be a priest upon His throne." Zechariah 6:13 . Again: "He made intercession for the transgressors." Isaiah 53:12.

Thus, as we come to the end of this prophecy written by the Hebrew prophet Isaiah, we see that the grand and glorious climax of it all is The Messiah, **Yeshua <u>Ha-Mashiach</u>**, as He stands before the Father today, pleading for all of us who have accepted Him as our personal Saviour and Redeemer. This is the plan of salvation given by the Lord to the Hebrew people. Friend, let us turn our eyes and our hearts to the God of Israel, who so loved us and gave to us His Messiah, The Redeemer, The Suffering Servant of God, that we might have eternal life. Amen.

CHAPTER 6

Prophecies of The Messiah and their Fulfillment

OUR JEWISH PEOPLE have waited for many generations for the coming of The Messiah. Many have hoped and prayed for deliverance by Him, to no avail, believing that He has tarried too long and will not come. However, there are some of our Jewish people who believe that He has tarried and He will come. The vast majority have lost hope and have strayed away from the religion of Israel, because they have lost faith in God. Our Jewish people should not have lost faith in God for the LORD has not left us in ignorance concerning The Messiah. He not only gave us prophecies concerning The Messiah but He also recorded their fulfillments in the Holy Scriptures.

Therefore, there is no need for any of us to be in ignorance concerning The Messiah. In the Holy Scriptures there is recorded about 300 points of prophecy concerning the coming of The Messiah. God, through the angel Gabriel, made known to the Hebrew prophet Daniel the year when The Messiah would come. Centuries later The Messiah came in the very year appointed by God.

This is no accident. When the Hebrew prophets wrote of these prophecies, they did so under the inspiration of God. This is confirmed in the **Holy Scriptures,** and by our **Sages, Prophets, and Rabbis,** who tell us that the writings were directed by God. Thus, we have not followed cunningly devised fables, but the truth, which God Himself set forth in His Holy Word. The only people who are not aware of these great happenings are those who have neglected to study God's word to find for themselves what is truth and what is error.

Ask God to open your heart and mind as we study the Holy Scriptures to see what He has foretold and has caused to come to pass concerning The Messiah. In Genesis 49:10, the Holy Scriptures state, "The scepter shall not part from Judah, nor a lawgiver from between his feet; until Shiloh comes, and unto Him shall the gathering of the people be." "Shiloh is another appelation [name] of The Messiah". Our Sages, Prophets, and Rabbis have known throughout the centuries that this Scripture verse refers to Him. We read these words in the Babylonian Talmud: "Rab said: The world was created only on David's account; Samuel said: On Moses' account; R. Johanna said: for the sake of The Messiah. What is his [The Messiah's] name? - The School of R. Shila said; His name is Shiloh, for it is written until Shiloh come (Gen. XLIX, 10)." **Sanhedrin** 98b, volume 2, p. 667, Soncino Press.

When God declared that the scepter would not depart from the tribe of Judah He meant that the kingdom of Judah would not depart until Shiloh, the Peace-giver came, and that the tribe of Judah would remain in tact until the coming of The Messiah. We Jews well remember the sad history of how we lost our homeland, our kingdom, and were driven out into all parts of the world. Our longest exile has lasted almost 2,000 years, and God foretold that we would not return as a true theocracy until the coming of The Messiah in the latter days.

The fact that the Jewish people lost their kingdom is one of the great signs that The Messiah has come once. Moses, under the inspiration of God, wrote, "The scepter shall not depart from Judah, nor a lawgiver from between his feet; until Shiloh come, and unto Him shall the gathering of the people be." Genesis 49:10. Here is proof that The Messiah has come, and that His next appearance will be His second coming. The Torah is so impressive in its simplicity that one need not be endowed with great intelligence to grasp its meaning. The Messiah - Shiloh - has come, and the aforementioned scripture verse substantiates it.

There are approximately 300 prophecies concerning the coming of The Messiah; for example, the Holy Scriptures tell us how, when, and where The Messiah would make His appearance. They also tell us His name, and the manner in which He will come. Let us examine a few of the prophecies that God has given us through our Hebrew prophets: "Behold the days shall come, saith the LORD, and I shall rise up unto David a righteous Shoot [or Scion], and a righteous King shall reign, and He shall prosper, and He shall execute judgement and shall do justice in the earth. In His days Judah shall be saved, and Israel shall dwell safely; and this shall be His name by which He shall be called: THE LORD OUR RIGHTEOUSNESS." Jeremiah 23:5,6.(See Miachel Friedlander's rendering of Jeremiah 23:5,5.) The following Talmudic statement concerning Jeremiah 23:5,6 is worth noting: "[as regards] The Messiah—as it is written: And this is the name whereby he shall be called. The LORD is our righteousness [Jer. xxiii,6]." **Baba Bathra** 75b, p. 303, Soncino Press. Regarding the same prophecy the **Midrash** comments most significantly; "What is the name of King Messiah? R. Abba b. Kahana said: His name is 'the LORD', as it is stated,And this is the name whereby he shall be called. The LORD is our righteousness (Jer. 23,6)."—**Midrash Rabbah** on Lamentations, chapter 1, section 16, part 51, pp.135,136,Soncino Press.

The Bible, Talmud, and Midrash make it very clear that The Messiah is a divine being called "The LORD our righteousness." The fulfillment of this prophecy is recorded in the book of Matthew 12:23, and 21:9 [New Testament]. "And all the people were amazed, and said, Is this not the son of David? And the multitudes that went before, and that followed, cried, saying, Hosanna to the son of David: Blessed is He that cometh in the name of the LORD; Hosanna in the highest."

Let us examine a prophecy that was recorded 700 years before its fulfillment, before The Messiah was to be born into this world , as our God told us how The Messiah would appear. "For a male child is born to us, a Son is given to us; and the government shall be upon His shoulders; and His name shall be called Wonderful Counselor, Mighty God, Everlasting Father, Prince of Peace [Pele-joez-el-gibbor-Abi-ad-sar-Shalom]. There shall be no end to the increase of [His] government and peace upon the throne of David, and over His kingdom, to stabilize it, and to establish it in judgment and in justice from this time and unto eternity: The zeal of the LORD of hosts will do this."Isaiah 9:5,6. Luke 2:8-11 is the fulfillment of this prophecy, "And the shepherds were in the same region, lodging in the fields, and keeping watch by night over their flock. And behold, an angel of the LORD stood by them, and the glory of the LORD shone around them; and they feared with great fear. And the angel said to them: Do not fear; for behold,I announce good news [gospel] of great joy to you, which shall be for all people; because there was born to you today a Saviour, who is The Messiah the LORD, in the city of David."

Look at a prophecy in Psalms 2:2,4,7. It shows who The Messiah is and what His relationship is to God. "The kings of the earth set themselves, and the rulers take counsel together against the LORD, and against His Anointed [Hebrew: **Mashiac**, 'Messiah']. He that sitteth shall laugh: the LORD shall have them in derision... I will declare the decree: the

LORD hath said unto Me, Thou art My Son; this day have I begotten Thee." The Talmud says: "Our Rabbis taught, The Holy One, blessed be He, will say to The Messiah, the son of David (May he reveal himself speedily in our days!) Ask of Me anything, and I will give it to thee, as it is said, I will tell them of the decree,etc. This day I have begotten thee, ask of Me and I will give thee the nations for thy inheritance." **Sukkah 52a,** p.247, Soncino Press. We are also informed; "The application of the term 'son of God' to The Messiah rests chiefly on Ps.ii,7 and the other Messianic passages quoted above."—**The Jewish Encyclopedia**, volume 11, p.461, article **"Son of God"**. We find God the Father calling The Messiah, "My Son." The Messiah is divinely referred to as the Son of God. This was confirmed a 1000 years after Psalm 2 was written. In the historical record it is stated that when The Messiah came out of the water after being immersed by John, " Lo, a voice from heaven, saying, This is My beloved Son, in whom I am well pleased." Matthew 3:17. The name "Yashua" was given to The Messiah because God proposed to deliver His people from the penalty and power of sin through The Messiah.[Hebrew: Yashua Ha Mashiach].

When the angel of the LORD spoke concerning Mary [Miriam] and the birth of The Messiah as her son, he said: "The one in her (womb) is begotten of the Holy Spirit. And she shall bear a Son, and thou shalt call His name Yeshua, for He shall save His people from their sins."Matthew 1: 23. We have studied the prophecy revealing the year of The Messiah's appearing among God's chosen people. That prophecy was given more than 500 years before His appearing took place. It is recorded in these words concerning the 70 prophetic weeks allotted to Jerusalem and the Jewish nation: "Know thou and understand thou: From the going forth of a commandment to restore and to rebuild Jerusalem unto Prince Messiah [shall be] seven weeks and 62 weeks." Daniel 9:25. As explained in the chapter, "The 490 Year Prophecy," we showed that according to Ezra the seventh chapter, the commandment, or decree, for the Jewish people to complete the restoration and rebuilding of Jerusalem went forth in the fall of 457 B.C.E. See Ezra 6: 14. We note that from the going forth of this decree would be seven weeks [of years] and 62 weeks [of years], which gives us a total of 69 weeks. Since there are seven years in a week of years, seven times 69 would give us 483 years. Also, according to Ezekiel 4:6 and Numbers 14:34, in Bible prophecy a symbolic day represents a year. Thus, these 483 prophetic days represent 483 literal years. Adding the 483 years to the autumn of 457 B.C.E.,we come to the autumn of 27 C.E. [commonly known as 27 A.D.]. In the fall of 27 C.E. we find Yeshua, The Messiah, coming to the river Jordan. Notice this record of the fulfillment of this time prophecy: "Then Yeshua comes from Galilee to John at the Jordan to be immersed by him. But he [John] forbade Him, saying: I have need to be immersed by Thee, and comest Thou to me? And answering, Yeshua said to him: Permit [it] now; for thus it becomes us to fulfill all righteousness. Then he permits Him. And having been immersed, Yeshua went up immediately from the water; and lo, the heavens were opened, and He saw the Spirit of God descending as a dove coming upon Him. And behold, a voice out of the heavens, saying: This is My beloved Son, in whom I have been well pleased." Matthew 3: 13-17.

Afterward, John "sees Yeshua coming toward him, and he says: Behold the Lamb of God; the One bearing the sin of the world." John 1:29. Thus was fulfilled the 483-year time prophecy indicating when The Messiah would appear to begin His public ministry of three and a half years, after which time He would offer Himself as a sacrifice for the sins of the people. The Talmud seems to substantiate the fact that The Messiah should have come 4,000 years after creation. Note this statement: "The Tanna debe Eliyuahu teaches : The world is to exist 6,000 years. In the first 2,000 years there was desolation; 2,000 years the Torah flourished; and the next 2,000 years is the Messianic era, but through our many iniquities all these years have been lost." **Sanhedrin** 97a and 97b volume 2, p. 657, Soncino Press. Editorial footnote No.10 states: "i.e., Messiah will come within that period." Footnote No.11 "He should have come at the beginning of the last two thousand years; the delay is due to our sins." According to God's Holy Word, The Messiah came almost 2,000 years ago, and according to the Talmud,He came at the time predicted in the Holy Scriptures.

Notice these prophecies and their fulfillments:

Prophecy: "Rejoice greatly, O daughter of Zion; and shout, O daughter of Jerusalem;behold thy King shall come to thee, just and having salvation: He [is] lowly and riding upon the ass, and upon a colt, a foal of an ass." Zechariah 9:9. In the

Talmud it is said concerning the Temple: "Yet Zechariah, prophesying in the days of the second (Temple), proclaimed Rejoice greatly, O daughter of Zion; shout, O daughter of Jerusalem; behold, thy king cometh unto thee! he is just, and having salvation; lowly , and riding upon an ass, and upon a colt the foal of an ass (Zech. 9: 9)."- **Sanhedrin** 99a, volume 2, p.669, Soncino Press. "Similarly it will be with the latter Redeemer," says a Midrashic treatise, "as it is stated, Lowly ,and riding upon an ass (Zech. 9)." -**Midrash Rabbah**,on Ecclesiastes, chapter 1,section 9,part 1, p.33, Soncino Press.

Fulfillment: "And the disciples, going and doing as Yeshua had directed them, brought the ass and the colt and they put upon them their garments; and He sat on them. And the very large crowd strewed their garments in the road, and others cut branches from the trees and strewed [them] in the road. And the crowds going before Him and the ones following Him cried out, saying: Hosanna to the son of David; blessed be the One coming in the Lord's name; hosanna in the highest (places)." Matthew 21:6-9.

Prophecy: " I said unto them, if ye think good, give me my price;and if not, forbear. So they weighed for my price 30 pieces of silver." Zechariah 11:12.

Fulfillment: " Then one of the twelve, called Judas Iscariot, went unto the chief priests, and said unto them, What will ye give me, and I will deliver Him unto you? And they covenanted with him for thirty pieces of silver." Matthew 26:14, 15.

Prophecy: "For [it was] not an enemy [who] reproached Me, or I could have borne it; neither did My adversary magnify himself against Me, or I could have hidden Myself from him. But [it was] thou,a man as My equal, My companion and My familiar friend, when we took sweet counsel together [and] we walked with the crowd in the house of God." Psalm 55: 12-14. Also Psalm 41:10; Zechariah 13:6.

Fulfillment: " And immediately approaching Yeshua, he [Judas Iscariot] said: Hail, Rabbi, and he affectionately kissed Him. And Yeshua said to him: Friend, on what [mission] art

thou? Then, approaching, they laid hands on Yeshua and seized
Him." Matthew 26:49,50.

Prophecy: " And the LORD said unto me, Cast it unto the
potter: a goodly price that I was prised at of them. And I took
the thirty pieces of silver and cast them to the potter in the
house of the Lord." Zechariah 11:13.

Fulfillment: "And he [Judas] cast down the pieces of silver
in the Temple, and departed, and went and hanged himself.
And the chief priests took the silver pieces. And they took
counsel, and bought with them the potter's field." Matthew
26:5,7. See also verses 9,10.

Prophecy: "Smite the shepherd,and the sheep shall be
scattered." Zechariah 13:7.

Fulfillment: "All the disciples forsook Him [Yeshua], and
fled." Matthew 26:56. See Mark 14: 27.

Prophecy: "He [Yeshua] was despised and rejected of
men; a Man of sorrows, and acquainted with grief: and we hid
as it were our faces from Him; He was despised, and we
esteemed Him not." Isaiah 53:3.

Fulfillment: " He [Yeshua] came unto His own, and His
own received Him not." John 1: 11.

Prophecy: " False witnesses rose up against Me; they
questioned [Me] about that which I did not know." Psalm
35:11.

Fulfillment: " And the chief priests and the whole
Sanhedrin sought false witnesses against Yeshua that they
might put Him to death, and they did not find many false
witnesses coming forward. And later two, approaching said:
This man said: I am able to destroy the Temple of God and in
three days build (it)." Matthew 26:59.

Prophecy: "I gave My back to the smiters, and My cheeks
to them that plucked off the hair; I hid not My face from shame
and spitting." Isaiah 50:6.

Fulfillment: " Then did they spit in His face, and buffeted Him;and others smote Him with the palms of their hands." Matthew 26: 67.

Prophecy: " He was oppressed, and was afflicted, and He opened not His mouth: He was brought as the lamb to the slaughter, and dumb as a sheep before its shearers, He opened not His mouth." Isaiah 53:7.

Fulfillment: " And when He was accused of the chief priests and elders, He answered nothing. Then said Pilate unto Him, hearest thou not how many things they witness against thee? And He answered him never a word; insomuch that the governor marvelled greatly." Matthew 27:12-14.

Prophecy: " And He [was] wounded on account of our transgressions, He was bruised on account of our iniquities;the chastisement of our peace [was] upon Him,and by means of His stripes we have been healed." Isaiah 53:5.

Fulfillment: " Having scourged Yeshua, he [Pilate] delivered [Him] that He might be crucified. Then the soldiers, having plaited a crown of thorns, they placed [it] upon His head," etc. Matthew 27:26,29.

Prophecy: " My knees are week through fasting; and My flesh faileth of fatness." Psalm 109:24.

Fulfillment: " And He bearing His cross went forth." John 19:17. "They led forth Him [Yeshua], [and] seizing Simon, a certain Cyrenian coming from the field, they placed on him the cross to carry behind Yeshua." Luke 23:26.
The Messiah was then so weak that His knees gave way under the weight of the heavy cross. So they had to put it upon another to bear.

Prophecy: " The assembly of the wicked inclosed Me: they pierced My hands and My feet." Psalm 22:17. "And they shall gaze at Me whom they have pierced through." Zechariah 12:10. "And one shall say unto Him: What are these wounds between Thy hands?" Then He shall answer: "Those with which I was wounded in the house of my friends." Zechariah 13:6.

Fulfillment: " Therefore, he [Pilate] delivered Him [Yeshua] to them that He might be crucified; and He, bearing the cross by Himself, went forth to the place called that of the skull, which is called Golgotha in Hebrew, where they crucified Him... For these things happened that the scripture might be fulfilled: Not a bone of Him shall be broken. And, again, another scripture says: They shall gaze at Him whom they pierced through." John 19:16-18,36,37.

Prophecy: "(He) made intercession for the transgressors." Isaiah 53:12.

Fulfillment: "And Yeshua said: O Father, forgive them, for they do not know what they are doing." Luke 23:34.

Prophecy: " I became also a reproach unto them: when they looked upon Me they shook their heads." Psalm 109:25.

Fulfillment: " And they that passed by reviled Him [Yeshuah], wagging their heads." Matthew 27:39.

Prophecy: " He trusted on the LORD that He would deliver Him: let Him deliver Him, seeing He delighted in Him." Psalm 22:8.

Fulfillment: " Likewise also the chief priests mocking Him [Yeshua], with the scribes and elders, said,... He trusted in God; let Him deliver Him now , if He will have Him." Matthew 27:41,43.

Prophecy: " They look and stare upon Me." Psalm 22:18.

Fulfillment: " And the people stood beholding." Luke 23:35.

Prophecy: " He [was] brought as the lamb to the slaughter. The travail of His soul He shall see; their iniquities He shall bear." Isaiah 53:7,11.

Fulfillment: "He [Yeshua] has appeared for the putting away of sin by means of the sacrifice of Himself so also The Messiah, having been offered once to bear the sins of many, will appear the second time, without sin, to those expecting Him for salvation." Hebrews 9:26,28.

Prophecy: " For Thou wilt not abandon My soul to the grave; neither wilt Thou suffer Thine Holy One to see corruption." Psalm 16:10.

Fulfillment: "David...seeing beforehand, spoke concerning the resurrection of The Messiah,that neither was He left in the grave, nor His flesh saw corruption. This Yeshua The Messiah God has raised up, of which all we are witnesses." Acts 2:29-32. "And answering,the angel said to the women: Fear ye not;for I know that ye seek Yeshua, the one having been crucified. He is not there, for He has been raised up, as He said. Come ye and see the place where He lay. And going quickly, tell ye His disciples that he was raised up from the dead and going away quickly from the tomb, with fear and great joy, they race to report to His disciples. And, behold, Yeshua met them,saying: Hail! And, approaching,they held His feet and worshiped Him." Matthew 28:5-9.

In this chapter we have studied some of the most wonderful prophecies concerning The Messiah, and their fulfillments. We must bear in mind that there are over 300 points of prophecy concerning Him. Thus, we have only begun to touch the vast number of prophecies that are in the Bible to prove that The Messiah has come and that He was none other than the one named by God Himself, Yeshua The Messiah. Yeshua has had such a marvelous influence upon the world that He has split the centuries in two divisions. Everything before Him is dated B.C.E. by the Jewish people, and B.C. by the Gentiles. Everything after Him is dated C.E. by the Jewish people, and A.D. by the Gentiles. Thus, so powerful a figure was The Messiah, the Son of the living God, that everything dates before Him or after Him. All history revolves about His name.

He, who died for our sins that through Him we might have eternal life, is the greatest figure today in all human history. The greatest of men are but pigmies in comparison to Yeshua The Messiah. All prophecy points to the soon return of our Jewish Messiah, who will not come again to die for our sins, but to take us into His eternal kingdom, where we shall never know of death, and where sin and sinners will be no more.

CHAPTER 7

Can We Identify The Messiah?

As a foundation for this chapter we will first contemplate on the many names of God. The angels in heaven adore Him and praise His name. Continually they cry, "Holy, Holy, Holy, is the LORD of hosts." Isaiah 6:3. If these holy, sinless beings sing praises to the Most High, how much more should we, sinful and undone creatures of the dust come before Him in humility.

The name of our God is expressive of His character. This was clearly revealed by Moses centuries ago: "And the LORD, descended in the cloud, and stood with him there, and proclaimed the name of the LORD. And the LORD passed by before him, and proclaimed, The LORD, the LORD God, merciful and gracious, longsuffering, and abundant in goodness and truth." Exodus 34:5,6.

May we know the actual name of our heavenly Father? This is an old question, of course. It was asked a long time ago. "What is His name, and what is His son's name, if thou canst tell?" Proverbs 30:4.

Certainly the Ruler of the universe has a name. We should approach this theme with deep humility of heart and mind. We should remember that the name of our God is"Holy" (Isaiah 57:15); it is "glorious" (Nehemiah 9:5); it is "excellent" (Psalm 148:13); it is "reverend" (Psalm 111:9).

There are some who contend that there is but one name, and one name only, by which the God of heaven should be known, and that is the Tetragrammaton (YHWH) rendered Lord, God, or JEHOVAH in some translations. It is readily conceded that the Tetragrammaton is undoubtedly the most distinctive name of the Most High, but it is not the only name of the great Creator. The Tetragrammaton was regarded by the Hebrews as a very 'sacred' name. During the last three centuries B.C.E., they began to fear to take it upon their lips. We, too, will do well to approach the study of this wonderful name with a sense of sacred awe.

It will be noted that there are quite a number of names and titles ascribed to the Most High. All texts used in the following outline are from the Hebrew Bible.

He is the LORD   (YHWH). "I am the LORD, that is my name." The Eternal One. "Thus saith the LORD the maker thereof." Isaiah 42:8. "The LORD is His name." Jeremiah 33:2.

He is Yah. Short poetic form of YHWH. "Sing unto God [Elohim], sing praises to His name: extol Him that rideth upon the heavens by His name Jah [**Yah**] and rejoice before Him." Psalm 68:5; Isaiah 38:11 in Hebrew.

He is Adonai (LORD). "O LORD [**Adonai**], hear, O LORD [**Adonai**], forgive, ... because Thy name is called upon Thy city and upon Thy people." Daniel 9:19.

He is Elohim (Great Ones). "God [Elohim] said to David...: 'In this house, and in Jerusalem, ...will I put My name forever.' " 2 Chronicles 33:7. "Great is our God [Elohim] above all gods." 2 Chronicles 2:4.

He is Adonai Yahew (LORD Eternal). "I will sanctify My great name...and the nations shall know that I am the LORD [YHWH], saith the LORD GOD [**Adonai YHWH**]." Ezekiel 36:23.

He is Yahweh Elohim (Eternal God). "The LORD God [YHWH 'Elohim] formed man of the dust of the ground." Genesis 2:7.

He is Yahweh Adonai (GOD the Lord). "Thou, O GOD the Lord [YHWH 'Adonai], deal with me for thy name's sake." Psalm 109:21.

He is Yah Yahweh (Yah the LORD). "GOD the LORD [Yah YHWH], is my strength and song." Isaiah 12:2; 26:4.

He is El Shaddai   (God Almighty). "I appeared unto Abraham, unto Isaac, and unto Jacob, as God Almighty [**'El Ahaddai**]." Exodus 6:3 see Genesis 17:1.

He is Elohei ha 'elohim (God of gods). "The LORD
[YHWH] your God ['Elohim]. He is God of gods ['Elohei ha
'elohim], Lord of lords ['Adonai ha-'adonim], the great God,
the mighty, and the awful," etc..Deuteronomy 10:17.

He is Eheye (The self-existing or Everlasting One). "And
Moses said unto God ['Elohim], 'Behold when I come unto the
children of Israel, and shall say unto them: The God ['Elohei]
of your fathers has sent me unto you: and they shall say unto
me: What is His name? what shall I say unto them?' And God
['Elohim] said unto Moses: 'I AM THAT I AM' ['Ehyeh
'asher 'Ehyeh]; and He said: 'Thus shall you say unto the
children of Israel: I AM ['Ehyeh] hath sent me unto you.' "
That is, He was, and is, and ever shall be. Exodus 3:13.

It is evident from the above that the God of heaven, the true
God, revealed Himself by several different names through the
centuries. It is also true,however, that the Tetragrammaton was
the most distinctive name by which He was known to the
people who faithfully served Him in ancient days. None of the
nations surrounding Israel, so far as is known, used the
Tetragrammaton as a name for their gods. They did use
'el,'elah,'elohim, and 'adon in reference to their deities. And
'elohim was used when referring to their heathen gods (2
Chronicles 32:13).

This subject, no doubt, will not only be of deep interest, but
will also be dear to the heart of all. John 5:43 says: "I am come
in My Father's name." But what did The Messiah mean when
He made this statement? We read again: "Behold, I send an
angel before thee, to keep thee by the way, and to bring thee
unto the place which I have prepared. Take heed of him,and
hearken unto his voice; be not rebellious against him; for he
will not pardon your transgression; for My name is in him."
Exodus 23:20,21.

It should be particularly noted that this angel has power to
pardon sins, which could not apply to an ordinary angel or
mortal man. It could be true of none other than a divine being-
The Messiah Himself. So our heavenly Father says concerning
Him: "My name is in Him." The Messiah says: "I am come in
My Father's name." In the English translation of the Bible The
Messiah is called "Jesus" (a transliteration of the Hebrew name
Yeshua') and our heavenly Father is called "God." When we

place the English words "God" and "Jesus" side by side, it is not easy to see fully the relationship between Father and Son. We do not clearly see the Father's name in the Son,nor the Son's name in the Father, because one is spelled "G-o-d" and the other is spelled "J-e-s-u-s." There is not even one letter alike in these two names. As a result, the average Bible student is perplexed when he reads: "I am come in My Father's name," and "My name is in Him."

Let us seek to discover the meaning and endeavor to see the beauty of these texts: "I am come in My Father's name" and "My name is in Him." In Matthew 6:9 we read these opening words of the prayer which The Messiah taught His disciples: "After this manner therefore pray ye: Our Father which art in heaven, hallowed be Thy name." If The Messiah teaches us to pray: "Our Father, hallowed be Thy name"; and He states, "I am come in My Father's name"; and the Father says concerning the Son, "My name is in Him," then ought we not to search the Scriptures and seek to ascertain the actual name of both the Father and the Son?

There is a text in the Bible which should prove of real value to us. This is found in Proverbs 30:4, it reads: "Who hath ascended up into heaven, and descended? Who hath gathered the wind in His fists? Who hath bound the waters in His garment? Who hath established all the ends of the earth? What is His name,and what is His Son's name, if thou knowest?" Today, strangely enough,very few people can answer this important question. Rightly understood, it is answered in the Word of God. The question is asked in the Scriptures: "What is His name, and what is His Son's name, if thou knowest?"

In this chapter our first point will be to establish the distinctive name of God the Father and then to establish the name of His Son, The Messiah, as the Redeemer of men. In giving consideration to the name of God, let us remember the earlier part of this study,i.e., that God has been known through the centuries by many names-**El,Elohim, Adonai, El Shaddai**, etc., and that the distinctive name by which He was known to His own people was the Tetragrammton (YHWH, or **Yahweh**), as has already been mentioned. No other nation, so far as is known, ever used this name when referring to its gods. It is this distinctive name which we shall now consider. In the Hebrew Bible the Tetragrammaton is used 5,989 times in its full form (see **The Jewish Enclyclopedia**, vol.12,p.118, col.2,art. "Tetragrammaton"). The pronunciation of this name has been perverted due to the fact that in the eighth century the Masorete Hebrew scholars believed the name of God too sacred to be spoken and therefore, decided to add to it the vowel points of the name 'Adonai ("Lord") to let the reader know that he should say that instead of the Tetragrammaton when reading the Bible aloud.

When the Bible was translated from the Hebrew into English, some translators rendered the Tetragrammaton as "Jehovah" because the Masorete scholars had given the Hebrew word the vowel points of 'Adonai. This rendering of the word as "Jehovah" in English is a mistake. The Tetragrammaton has a very definite meaning as we shall discover. In Hebrew the name "Adonai" means "lord" or "master." Thus, the only way the term "Adonai" should be translated into English is "Lord" or "Master." There are also places where it is used in the Bible in reference to The Messiah, as in Psalm 110. The name Adonai is a term used by the Jewish people instead of the Tetragrammaton, but this,too, is incorrect. As a result of this change, the English translators followed the Jewish pattern and instead of transliterating the name Yahweh into English, simply translated it as "Lord" (Adonai). In other words, the English translators of the King James version and other versions did exactly what the Masoretes had done.

As we read the English Bible today, we will find that where the Tetragrammaton appears in the Hebrew text, either "Lord" or "God" appears in large and small capital letters. When they translated 'Adonai they did not use all capital letters; it appears in one capital and three lower case letters as "Lord". When they translated 'El or 'Elohim, the Hebrew terms for God, they did not use all capital letters;thus it appears in one capital and lower case letters as "God" With this in mind, when we read the Bible in English we can know that wherever "Lord" or "God" appears in a large capital and small letters, it is where the Tetragrammaton appears in the Hebrew text. The term 'Elohim in the Hebrew Scriptures means Gods, the mighty ones, or deity, and it is applied to heathen gods, as well as to the one and only selfexistent God of heaven. The term 'Elohim is more a generic form, a general term, having a wide or general application. Let us notice how the generic term 'Elohim is used in the Bible. Observe not only 'Elohim, but also El and Elah.

"Judah hath profaned the holiness of the Lord, which He loveth and hath married the daughter of a strange god(El)." Malachi 2:11. "But the Lord God (**Elohim**) is the true God (**Elohim**), He is the living God (**Elohim**), and the everlasting King; at His wrath the earth trembleth, and the nations are not able to abide His indignation. Thus shall ye say unto them: 'The gods (**"elahayya'**) that have not made the heavens and the earth, these shall perish from the earth, and from under these heavens.'" Jeremiah 10:10,11. "It shall be, if thou shalt forget the LORD thy God (**'Elohim**), and walk after other gods (**'elohim**), and serve them, and worship them, I forewarn you this day that ye shall surely perish." Deuteronomy 8:19. Here we see how **Elohim** is used of the true God and also of the false gods. To substantiate the fact that God, or **Elohim**, is a generic term we quote from the following sources: In the **Encyclopedia of Religion and Ethics**, edited by James Hastings,we read as follows: "The names used for God were significant. **Elohim** was the generic term for Deity. **Jahweh** (Yahweh) the personal name of the God of Israel."-volume 6, p. 253, Chas. Scribner & Sons. The word "generic" means having a wide or general application. **The Encyclopaedia Biblica**, edited by T.K. Cheyne and J.S. Black, explains it in these words: "The plural (**Elohim**) serves sometimes to denote the heathen gods (Ex.9:1;12: 12; 20:3, etc.) or images of gods (Ex.20:23,etc.) but mostly to denote a single god (or image of a god e.g., Exodus 32:1, most probably also Genesis 31:30,32),whether a heathen deity (e.g., 1 Samuel 5:7,of Dagon; 1 Kings 11:5)," etc,-volume 3, column 3324, article "Names of God" Watts and Company.

To illustrate how the term "God" may be used in the generic or general form, note the following examples: (1) A heathen may worship a god of stone, but a follower of the Bible will worship the self-existent God of Heaven. (2) The name of this God is **Yahweh**, which means the "self-existent One." (3) Praise the God of Abraham, Isaac, and Jacob, whose name is the Lord (Tetragrammaton). (4) Our God is a God of gods, whose name is the Lord. Thus we see how to use the term "God," and how we use His name.

A widely used reference of long standing among us gives these facts: "Of the names of God in the Old Testament, that which occurs most frequently (6,823 times) is the so-called Tetragrammaton, YHWH, (???) the distinctive personal name of the God of Israel. This name is commonly represented in

modern translations by the form 'Jehovah,' which, however, is
a philological impossibility (see JEHOVAH). This form has
arisen through attempting to pronounce the consonants of the
name with the vowels of Adonai (??? ='Lord'), which the
Masorites have inserted in the text, indicating thereby that
Adonai was to be read (as a 'keri perpetum') instead of
YHWH."-**The Jewish Encyclopedia**, volume 9, p.160, article
" Names of God."

This reveals some interesting data concerning that name of
the self-existing God. We might ask, "What is the significance
of the true name of God?" For the answer, we quote again
from the same source: "In appearance, YHWH (???') is the
third person singular imperfect 'kal' of, the verb ?? ('to be'),
meaning, therefore, 'He is,' or 'He will be,' or, perhaps, 'He
lives; the root idea of the word being, probably, 'to blow,' 'to
breathe,' and hence, 'to live.' With this explanation agrees the
meaning of the name given in Exodus 3:14, where God is
represented as speaking, and hence as using the first person-'I
Am' (???, from ?? the later equivalent of the archaic stem ??).
The meaning would, therefore, be 'He who is self-existing,
self-sufficient,' or, more concretely, 'He who lives.' There is
no doubt that the idea of life was intimately connected with the
name YHWH from the early times. He is the living God, as
contrasted with the lifeless gods of the heathen, and He is the
source and author of life. So familiar is this conception of God
to the Hebrew mind that it appears in the common formula of
an oath, 'hai YHWH' (='as YHWH lives'; Ruth 3:13; 1 Samuel
14:45;etc.).Ibid. "If the explanation of the form above given be
the true one, the original pronunciation must have been
Yahweh (???) From this the contracted form Jah or Yah (??) is
most readily explained," etc.-Ibid., pp. 160, 161. We see,
therefore, that this distinctive name of God identifies Him as
being the "Eternal One," the "Self-existent One." This
immediately places Him in a category to which no other god
can attain. God was also referred to by the Tetragrammaton
early in the world's history as we see in this passage: "And to
Seth, to him also there was born a son; and he called his name
Enosh; then began men to call on the name of the LORD
(Tetragrammaton)." Genesis 4:26.

One well-known Jewish reference work says concerning
this name of God: "The Tetragrammaton of Four-Lettered
Name (???), which occurs 6,823 times, is by far the most
frequent name of God in the Bible. It is now pronounced

'adonai; but the church father Theodoret records that the Samaritans pronounced it as 'labe (labe), and Origen transcribes it as lae (lae), both pointing to an original vocalization yahveh."

"In course of time, as the tribes united into a nation, all other names were superseded by the Tetragrammaton, Yahveh; this process seems to have been completed by the middle of the 9th cent. B.C.E., after which time almost every royal name is compounded with Yahveh. During the Middle Ages, Christian students of Hebrew mistakenly read the four consonants of the Tetragrammaton with the vowels indicating the pronunciation 'adonai; they thereby arrived at the form YeHoVah, which has produced the name Jehovah for God. This name Jehovah, which still survives in Christian Bible translations and Christian prayer books, is actually a mistransliteration, and the word itself is meaningless."-**The Universal Jewish Encyclopedia,** volume 5, pp.6,7,article "God, Names of."

Regarding JAH (Yah), the contracted form of the Tetragrammaton, we read: "Sing unto God, sing praises to His name: extol Him that rideth upon the heavens by His name Jah, and rejoice before Him." Psalm 68:5. This name (a contraction of the Tetragrammaton) is seen in the last three letters in the word "Halleujah," a Hebrew word meaning "Praise ye Yah."

"It was the great prophets who put into the name **Yahweh** its universal significance, and who saw in the God of Israel the God of the whole universe. The more the prophets were brought to realize what God was in Himself, the more they realized that ultimately everything went back to Him. Nothing could be independent of the power and purpose of the everlasting God-'the Eternal.'"-**Harper's Bible Dictionary,** edited by Madeleine S.Miller and J.Lane Miller, p.230, Harper & Bros. The **New International Encyclopedia,** second edition, "The Samaritans seem to have continued longer than Jews to pronounce the holy name. Theodoret (Question xv in Exdum) declares that they pronounced it 'labe, i.e., Yave;and though **Shema** (the Name) has been substituted for it, there is unimpeachable evidence that even the Samaritans of today know that Yahweh was the original pronunciation."-volume 12,p.625. Notice this Bible text which shows that the Tetragrammaton is the name of the everlasting God. Genesis 21:33: "And Abraham planted a tamarisk tree in Beer-sheba and called there on the name of the Lord, the everlasting God." This is one of the earliest Bible references that speaks of an attribute of God by pointing to His eternal existence. It is He who is self-existent, He who is life, He who gives life.

People say, "Who can know God? He is out of our reach. He is just too far from us. Our minds just cannot comprehend God." Let us read again this statement which brings this out "Who hath ascended up into heaven, and descended? Who hath gathered the wind in His fists? Who hath bound the waters in His garment? Who hath established all the ends of the earth? What is His name, and what is His Son's name, if thou knowest? Every word of God is tried; He is a shield unto them that take refuge in Him. Add thou not unto His words, lest He reprove thee, and thou be found a liar." Proverbs 30:4-6. How clearly the Bible answers the question. The answer is given by The Messiah Himself in these words from the Holy Scriptures: "And yet the Son of man, descended from heaven, is the only one who has ever ascended into heaven. Indeed the Son of man must be lifted on high, even as Moses lifted up the (brazen) serpent in the desert, that everyone who believes in Him may have eternal life." John 3:13-15.

Let us answer the questions asked above: First study carefully the following outline: **Yeshua-His** name should be considered in its various forms, because other names than **"Yeshua"** are used in making reference to Him.

(1) His New Testament names:
(a) "Thou shalt call His name Jesus **(Yeshua)**." Matthew 1:21.
(b) "They shall call His name **Emmanuel,** which being interpreted (translated) is, God with us." Matthew 1:23.
(c) "His name is called **The Word of God.**" Revelation 19:13.
(d) "And the **Word** was made flesh, and dwelt among us, **the only begotten of the Father.**" John 1:14.
(e) "We have found The Messiah, which is being interpreted, **the Christ (Anointed One).**" John 1:41.

(2) His Old Testament names:
(a) "His name shall be called **Wonderful, Counsellor of the Mighty God, of the Everlasting Father, Prince of Peace.**" Isaiah 9:5.

That passage translated from Hebrew into Greek by scholarly Rabbis about the third century B.C.E. reads: "His name is called the **Messenger** of great counsel." LXX (Septuagint) Version, Samuel Bagster and Sons. This text was regarded as

Messianic by the ancient Rabbis. *The Targum of Isaiah* reads: "His name has been called from of old, **Wonderful Counsellor, Mighty God, He who lives forever, the Anointed One (or Messiah)."**

(b) "Behold, the man, whose name is **the Shoot."** Zechariah 6:12. "My servant the Shoot." Zechariah 3:8. In some English versions the Hebrew noun **tsemach** in these passages is rendered as **"Branch" or "Sprout."**

"I will raise unto David a righteous Shoot (Hebrew, **tsemach**), and he shall reign as King." Jeremiah 23:5 (J). In the Targum of Jeremiah this passage is interpreted thus: "I will raise up for David **The Messiah the Just."** The Talmudic sages, in their comment on Jeremiah 23:5, said: "This refers to **The Messiah,** of whom it also states, I will raise unto David a righteous shoot," etc. **Midrash Rabbah,** on Numbers, chapter 18, section 21, volume 2, p.734, Soncino Press.

(c) "And this is His name whereby He shall be called, **the Lord (YHWH) our righteousness."** Jeremiah 23:6. This text was also recognized in the Talmud as referring to The Messiah by many Hebrew sages of ancient times, notice:"(As regards) The Messiah-it is written: And this is the name whereby He shall be called, **The Lord is our righteousness."** -Baba Bathra 75b, volume 2, p.303 Soncino Press.

Over and over again Yeshua mentioned that the Father "sent" Him (John 4:24, 36); that He came "from heaven" (John 6:38); that His mission was to do, not His own will, but the will of His Father (John 4:30). This is revealed particularly in relation to the "name" of God. Yeshua said, "I am come in My Father's name" (John 5:43); "The works that I do in My Father's name bear witness of Me." (John 10:25). In prayer to God the Father He said: "I have manifested Thy name unto the men Thou gavest Me out of the world" (John 17:6); and, "I have declared unto them Thy name" (verse 26). It is evident, then, that there was an intimate relationship between The Messiah on earth and His Father in heaven. This relationship is beautifully expressed in His remarks "I and My Father are one" (John 10:30), and "I do always those things that please Him" (John 8:29).

In our own day, some still assert that there is but one name and one name only by which The Messiah, The Son of God, should be known, and that it is **Yashuah.** Let us observe that this is far from the truth and certainly not in harmony with the Holy Scriptures. Nowhere in the Bible, Hebrew or Greek, can one find such a name. Concerning The Son, we are instructed in the Hebrew Scriptures to: "Do homage to the Son, lest He be angry, and ye be lost on the way. Happy are all they that put their trust in Him." Psalm 2:12. "For whoso findeth me findeth life, and obtaineth favor of the Lord. But he that misseth me wrongeth his own soul; all they that hate me love death." Proverbs 8:35,36.

In the New Testament The Messiah, as The Son, declared: "I am the way, the truth, and the life." John 14:6. When the Son was born, He was not named by His earthly parents, but rather by His heavenly Father. Actually He was not named "Jesus" This name is a form which later came into the English language when the "Y" was replaced by the "J". He was not even named 'Iesous (pronounced Yesus), the Greek form of His name. As He was born of Hebrew parentage, His name would naturally be of Hebrew origin. Also, His name undoubtedly would indicate His mission. As we study this subject, we can be certain that The Messiah who was born almost 2,000 years ago is the true Messiah. We read in the Old Testament regarding The Messiah: "Rejoice greatly, O daughter of Zion; shout, O daughter of Jerusalem: behold, thy king cometh unto thee: he is just and having victory." Zechariah 9:9. The Hebrew word rendered as "victory" in this verse is translated as "salvation" in some English versions. "Behold, the Lord hath proclaimed unto the end of the world, Say ye to the daughter of Zion, Behold, Thy salvation cometh; behold, His reward is with Him, and His work before Him. And they shall call them, The holy people, The redeemed of the LORD." Isaiah 62:11, 12 .

Here we have The Messiah referred to in the Old Testament more than 700 years before He came the first time. This text, indicates that His name should bear relationship to His mission, for His purpose was to *SAVE* His people; that is, to save His own from sin in order that He might give them Eternal Life. Does the New Testament substantiate this Hebrew text? Listen to the words of The Messiah Himself: "And, behold, I come quickly;and My reward is with Me, to give every man according as His work shall be. I am the beginning and the end, the first and the last I am the root and the offspring of David, and the bright and morning star." Revelation 22:12,13,16. With these Scripture passages as a background, it, therefore,becomes easy to understand why the angel of God said to Joseph, a descendant of the ancient King David: "And she (Miriam) shall bring forth a son, and thou shalt call His name Jesus ('Iesous, the Greek transliteration of the Hebrew word **Yeshua,** which means "Saviour"): for He shall save His people from their sins." Matthew 1:21.

While the name **Yeshua** means "Salvation of the LORD," it means more than that. Just as **Yah** is a contraction of **Yahweh,** so **Yeshua'** is a contraction of **Yehoshua',** (see Numbers 13:16 and 1 Chronicles for examples of this un-abbreviated word) which means "Salvation of the LORD." Now we begin to see what the Son meant when He declared, "I am come in My Father's name" (John 5:43), and what the Father meant when He proclaimed, "My name is in Him." Exodus 23:21. In his translation **The New Testament in Modern Speech,** fourth edition, p. 4, The Pilgrim Press, Richard F. Weymouth in comment on Matthew 1:21 explains the name Jesus as follows: " The Greek form of 'Joshua,' which later (like 'Joram' 2 Kings ix. 14 for 'Jehoram' 2 Kings ix. 15;'Joash' 2 Kings xii. 20 for 'Jehoash' 2 Kings xii. 1; and 'Jonathan' most commonly for the 'Jehonathan' which we find in the Hebrew in 1 Sam.) is contracted from 'Jehoshua' or rather 'Yehoshua.' In the Hebrew of the O.T. only the uncontracted form occurs, and (in 1 and 2 Chron., Ezra, and Neh.) the contracted but altered 'Jeshua' which already approaches the later 'Jesus.' The full significance of the name 'Jesus' is seen in the original 'Yeho-shua,' which means 'Jehovah the Saviour' and not merely 'Saviour' as the word is often explained." Some of the world's leading Biblical scholars hold this view. See **Fausset's Bible Encyclopedia and Dictionary,** p.359; **The Century Dictionary and Cyclopaedia,** vol.3, p.3228. **Young's Analytical Concordance** to the Bible explains it as follows: Jesus, from Greek 'Iesous, from Hebrew **Yeshua,** Saviour." The **New Standard Dictionary,**p. 1318, word "Jesus" (Funk and Wagnalls Company, explains that the name "Jesus" in English has come down to us from **Jesus** in Latin, from 'Iesous in Greek, from **Yeshua'** in Hebrew, meaning "Jehovah is salvation." Whether we turn to sacred or secular authorities, we find this agreement regarding the name of The Messiah.

Thus in His life and even in His death He bore the name "Yeshua," for on His cross the words were written in Hebrew, Greek, and Latin:

"YESHUA OF NAZARETH
THE KING OF THE JEWS."
John 19:19.

Note that in some of the references given above the letter "J" is used in place of the original letter "Y" This is because in the Hebrew and the Greek there is no letter "J" in the alphabet. Hence,if we are to pronounce the names of the Father and the Son properly, we should use the original "Y." For example, when we pronounce the word "Hallelujah," we are actually saying "Hallelu-Yah" (Praise ye the LORD).

It is true that two Old Testament characters were given the name of "Joshua" because they were types of the real, the true,the original "Yeshua."One was the Joshua who succeeded Moses and led the children of Israel into the promised land. He was a type of the true Yeshua who will lead His people into the heavenly Canaan. The other one was Joshua, the high priest. He was a type of Yeshua, our great High Priest, who is making intercession for us at the present time in the heavenly sanctuary. God promised the second Joshua (Zechariah3:8) that He would, in the fulness of time, bring forth the Seed of David: "Hear now, O Joshua the high priest, thou and thy fellows that sit before thee; for they are men that are a sign; for,behold, I will bring forth My servant, the Shoot." Zechariah 3:8.

In the comment by Dr. A. Cohen,**The Twelve Prophets,** we read: "Modern as well as ancient interpreters agree in explaining **the Shoot** as the expected Messiah. The term designates Israel's ideal ruler (cf.Jer.xxiii. 5), and has quite naturally been applied to King Messiah 'The old tree of the Jewish State was dead, but the prophet foreshadows a new life through the springing up of a new shoot of David's house'(Barnes)." page 282, Soncino Press. To substantiate this commentary of Dr. Cohen, let us read a Biblical statement concerning The Messiah as the Shoot, who would come from the royal family of David whose father was Jesse: "And there shall come forth a shoot out of the stock of Jesse, and a twig shall grow forth out of his roots. And the spirit of the LORD shall rest upon him." Isaiah 11:1,2.

Since The Messiah and His family were Hebrews, His true name is stated thus: "The book of (the) generation of Yeshua Messiah, son of David, son of Abraham." Matthew 1:1. Literally translated, His name is "Salvation of the LORD, The Messiah." Yeshua, meaning Salvation, is pronounced Yeh-shoo-ah. **Mashiach** is the Hebrew word transliterated into English as "Messiah," which means the "Anointed One." Thus, if the full Hebrew name of The Messiah were translated, it would read: "Salvation of the LORD, the Anointed One." If His Hebrew name were TRANSLITERATED, it would read "**Yeshua** The Messiah." The reason why we do not readily see the Father's name in that of the Son is because the English New Testament was translated from the Greek. When the New Testament was written in Greek,they transliterated the Hebrew name Yeshua to the Greek name 'Iesous,which is pronounced "Yesus." Thus, the English translators TRANSLITERATED the Greek name into English as "Jesus."

Since the translators both TRANSLATED and TRANSLITERATED the name of The Messiah, it will be interesting to note from the diagram that the English name "Jesus" comes from the Hebrew, and the name "Christ" comes from the Greek. To illustrate this, we must spell into English the Hebrew and the Greek names.

Original Hebrew Name —YESHUA'
Greek TRANSLITERATION—YESOUS
English TRANSLITERATION— JESUS

Explanation of diagram: Since the Greek language has no "sh" sound, they had to make it an "s" sound. Since in the Greek many proper names end with an "s" sound, they changed the Hebrew "a" sound to an "s" sound. Thus the Hebrew YESHUA became the Greek 'IESOUS. Then in the early seventeenth century when the English language was modernized, the "Y" sound became a "J" sound. Thus the Greek 'Iesous became the English "Jesus." In the transliteration referred to above, no other form of name could have been achieved. The transliterations from Hebrew to Greek and from Greek to English have been well done.

Let us find how the translators arrived at the name "Christ." Note that the Hebrew name for the "Anointed" is **Mashiach** and the Greek name for the "Anointed" is **Christos.**

Hebrew Original -"Anointed One" = MASHIACH
English TRANSLITERATION -"Mashiach" = MESSIAH
English TRANSLATION -"Mashiach" = ANOINTED ONE
Greek Original -"Anointed One" = CHRISTOS
English TRANSLITERATION -"Christos" = CHRIST
English TRANSLATION -"Christos" = ANOINTED ONE

Thus **Yeshua Ha-Mashiach** in Hebrew means "Salvation The Anointed" in English. The name "Jesus The Christ" means the same thing because "Jesus" corresponds to **Iesous** in Greek, which is the equivalent of **Yeshua'** (Salvation) in Hebrew. And the word "Christ" corresponds to **Christos** (Anointed). Thus "Jesus" gets its meaning from the Hebrew word **Yeshua'** (Salvation) and "Christ" gets its meaning from the Greek term **Christos** (Anointed).

When the Hebrew Scriptures were translated into the Greek language by Jewish scholars during the third and second centuries B.C.E.,they rendered the Hebrew word **Mashiach** into Greek as **Christos**, which means "Anointed One," instead of transliterating **Mashiach** as **Messias**. And when the New Testament was written in Greek, the writers, following the precedent already set by Jewish scholars, continued to use the term **Christos** ("Anointed One") as the correct Hellenic term equivalent to the Hebrew word **Mashiach.** Therefore, when the Greek New Testament was translated into English, the term **Christos** was transliterated into our language as "Christ," so that it retains and preserves the meaning of the original Hebrew word **Mashiach** ("Anointed One"). A good example of this is seen in John 1:41, where Nathaniel is quoted as saying to Simon: "We have found the Messias, which is, being interpreted, The Christ." The woman at Jacob's well in Samaria likewise is quoted as saying: "I know that Messias cometh, which is called Christ." John 4:25.

To a person not versed in the translations of the Holy Scriptures from the Hebrew into the various other languages, the real meaning of the word **Mashiach** ("Messiah") has been largely lost sight of. Thus, when we read the English Bible, we fail to see the Father's name is in the Son. If as Jewish people, we had studied the Bible, both Old and New Testaments in the original languages, we would have discovered this, and thousands today would be better informed concerning our Jewish Messiah. They would have seen the relationship that exists between God the Father and the Son. Thus, we understand that in the plan of salvation, the LORD, the Father, sent His son, the divine Messiah, in His own name. When The Messiah came to this earth and took upon Himself human flesh, the LORD, the Father, sent His angel to declare The Messiah's name, "Yeshua." Since **Yeshua** means "Salvation of the LORD," we can now understand what The Messiah meant when He said, "I am come in My Father's name"; and what the Father meant when He said, "My name is in Him."

Recognizing the distinctive Hebrew names of the Father and the Son, we can now appreciate the beauty and the significance of the names of the Creator and His divine Son. We find also in their name as God the idea of self-existing life, for the Deity alone is the Eternal One, the Everlasting One.

We can more fully appreciate the words of the Son when He spoke these words: "The LORD possessed Me in the beginning of His way, before His works of old. I was set up from everlasting, from the beginning, or ever the earth was. Then I was by Him, as one brought up with Him: and I was daily His delight, rejoicing always before Him." Proverbs 8:22,23,30.

CHAPTER 8

The Passover Seder—
Is Anything Missing?

THE CONCEPT of freedom is heaven born . Bondage, compulsion, and force are incompatible with the character of our heavenly Father. It is not God's will or plan that one nation should enslave another. When the Egyptians treated Jacob's offspring as bondmen and bondwomen, God plagued that nation and their proud,tyrannical monarch. But despite the mighty manifestations of divine power, Pharaoh stubbornly refused to free Israel until the first-born of every unbelieving household throughout the vast realm of Egypt was laid low. After recovering from their fears of God's retributive judgments, the Egyptians pursued the Israelites, only to perish in the depths of the Red Sea. Even though the event transpired 35 centuries ago, the Jewish people everywhere to this day annually celebrate the Passover in commemoration of that miraculous deliverance from Egyptian bondage.

The **Passover** is commonly known as the *Festival of Freedom.* The present mode of its observance by the Jews, however, differs vastly from the manner in which the ancients celebrated it. The latter followed the precise instruction as given them by God through Moses. In order to grasp the full significance of the Passover and its profound and sublime symbolism, it is necessary to study the divine directions recorded in Holy Writ. A prayerful contemplation of this original instruction will reveal that the God who hates physical bondage, likewise detests the most pernicious and degrading slavery of all-that of spiritual bondage to sin. In the celebration of the Passover feast, the most essential feature was the Passover lamb. Before the divine decree against the firstborn of Egypt was carried out, God said to Moses: "Speak ye unto all the congregation of Israel, saying, In the tenth day of this month they shall take to them every man a lamb, according to the house of their fathers, a lamb for an house. And if the household be too little for the lamb,let him and his neighbor next unto his house take it according to the number of the souls; every man according to his eating shall make your count for the lamb."

"Your lamb shall be without blemish, a male of the first year: ye shall take it out from the sheep, or from the goats: And ye shall keep it up until the fourteenth day of the same month: and the whole assembly of the congregation of Israel shall kill it in the evening [that is, about 3 p.m.]. And they shall take of the blood, and strike it on the two side posts and on the upper door post of the houses, wherein they shall eat it. And they shall eat the flesh in that night, roast with fire, and unleavened bread; and with bitter herbs they shall eat it." Exodus 12: 3-8.

"And thus shall ye eat it; with your loins girded, your shoes on your feet, and your staff in your hand; and ye shall eat it in haste: it is the LORD'S passover." Exodus 12:11.

"And the blood shall be to you for a token upon the houses where ye are: and when I see the blood, I will pass over you, and the plague shall not be upon you to destroy you, when I smite the land of Egypt." Exodus 12:13.

"In one house shall it be eaten; thou shalt not carry forth ought of the flesh abroad out of the house; neither shall ye break a bone thereof." Exodus 12:4

The faithful carrying out of the above instruction involved these salient points:

(a) The Paschal lamb (or kid) was to be chosen on the tenth day of Abib, the first month, and it was to be kept apart until the fourteenth day of that month.

(b) The lamb was to be without blemish.

(c) It was to be killed the fourteenth day in late afternoon.

(d) The shed blood was to be sprinkled upon the doorposts of the home.

(e) The flesh of the animal was roasted with fire to be eaten that night.

(f) It was to be eaten with unleavened bread.

(g) Not a bone of it was to be broken.

It was imperative to comply with these divine directions. Indeed, it was a life-and-death question. Had the Israelites

disregarded in any particular the directions given them, they ,
together with the Egyptians, would have lost their first-born by
the hand of the destroyer. It was not their illustrious ancestry
or their ethnic identity that saved them from the tenth plague on
that eventful night of destiny. The Lord Himself had pointed
out to Israel the only way and means of escape: "And the blood
shall be to you for a token upon the houses where ye are: and
when I see the blood, I will pass over you, and the plague shall
not be upon you to destroy you, when I smite the land of
Egypt." Exodus 12: 13.

By their obedience, Israel gave evidence of their faith in the
great deliverance about to be accomplished for them. They
realized that they themselves had something to do in securing
the safety of their first-born. The token of blood had to be
placed upon their houses. That sign of blood was the sign of
protection that made every household of Israel secure.

Then the plague struck with crushing force. The heaven-
daring pride of Pharaoh was now humbled in the dust. The
king "rose up in the night,he,and all his servants, and all the
Egyptians; and there was a great cry in Egypt; for there was not
a house where there was not one dead. And he called for
Moses and Aaron by night, and said, Rise up, and get you forth
from among My people, both ye and the children of Israel; and
go, serve the LORD, as ye have said. Also take your flocks
and your herds, as ye have said, and be gone; and bless me
also. And the Egyptians were urgent upon the people, that they
might send them out of the land in haste: for they said, We be
all dead men." Exodus 12:30-33.

Israel became a free people-delivered by the manifest
power of God. The gratitude and faith in the hearts of the
people later found expression in the triumphant anthem of
thanksgiving recorded in Exodus 15. This song, which
commemorates the great deliverance of the Hebrew people,
testifies that God is the hope of all who trust in Him. The
Passover with all its essential features was to be celebrated by
Israel in no other place except the one which God Himself
designated. "Thou mayest not sacrifice the passover within
any of thy gates, which the LORD thy God giveth thee: But at
the place which the LORD thy God shall choose to place His
name in, there thou shalt sacrifice the passover at even, at the
going down of the sun, at the season that thou camest forth out
of Egypt." Deuteronomy 16:5,6.

For several centuries the observance of Israel's annual feasts was centered in whatever place their portable sanctuary was located. But after the first Temple was built in the reign of King Solomon (971-931 B.C.E.), Jerusalem was the designated place. "Unto his son will I give one tribe, that David My servant may have a light always before Me in Jerusalem, the city which I have chosen Me to put My name there." 1 Kings 11:36.

The question arises as to why our heavenly Father stressed the slaying of a lamb. It is obvious that He could have freed Israel from Egypt without requiring them to sprinkle the blood of a lamb upon the lintels and doorposts of their houses. He takes no delight in the shedding of blood for its own sake. Since God required the shedding of this innocent blood, it must be done. He designed to teach Israel a lesson of outstanding importance, which could not have been conveyed to them by any better means or method. The offering up of animal sacrifices constituted a major part of the Jewish ritual services. No sin could be atoned for without the shedding of blood. Every sacrifice required because of transgression revealed the sacred character of the law of God, the Ten Commandments, which the sinner had broken. To sin is to break the commandments, for it is written: "If a soul shall sin against any of the commandments of the Lord..." Leviticus 4:2. It was clearly stated: "Sin is the transgression of the law." 1 John 3:4. The death of the sacrificed animals pointed to the ultimate result of sin, eternal death.

That is why it was necessary on the *Day of Atonement,* which we refer to as **Yom Kippur,** for the high priest to take the atoning blood of the goat, slain as a sin-offering for the people, and "sprinkle it upon the mercy seat, and before the mercy seat (i.e., the cover of the ark)." Leviticus 16:15. Inside the ark of the covenant were kept the two tables of stone upon which God had written with His own finger His law of Ten Commandments. The violation of any precept of that law was sin, and the penalty for transgression was death. The sprinkling of the blood of the animal slain as the sin-offering for the people signified it had died to pay the penalty for their transgression of that sacred law inside the ark.

When man sinned, he came under the power of death, for we read: "The soul that sinneth, it shall die." Ezekiel 18:4. "For the wages of sin is death..." Romans 6:23. Inasmuch as "there is none that doeth good, no, not one" Psalm 53:4, "All

have sinned, and come short of the glory of God" Romans
3:23; the entire human race is under this sentence of death.
"There is no man that sinneth not." 1 Kings 8:46; 2 Chronicles
6:36. "For there is not a righteous man upon earth,that doeth
good, and sinneth not." Ecclesiastes 7:20 . Were it not for the
goodness and mercy of God, all would be plunged into
hopeless despair; all would be doomed to misery and eternal
extinction. With the sacrificial system as an object lesson, God
taught Israel that a way had been provided whereby the
demands of His broken law could be satisfied and at the same
time mercy could be extended to the guilty sinner. Moses
wrote concerning this substitutionary death: "For the life of the
flesh [of the animal sacrificed] is in the blood: and I have given
it to you upon the altar to make an atonement for your souls:
for it is the blood that maketh an atonement for the soul."
Leviticus 17:11. In this brief verse God declared that the shed
blood of the innocent animal victim would make atonement for
the guilt of the soul. His infinite compassion and pity for the
fallen race that had moved Him to conceive a plan whereby
man might be redeemed. Every slain offering was a vivid
representation of the great Sacrifice by The Messiah, whose
vicarious death would atone for the guilt of one who had
broken God's law. His death confirmed and upheld the
authority of that law and made it possible for God to extend
mercy and forgiveness to the believing, repentant sinner.

Since God's law is as sacred as Himself, only one equal
with Himself could make atonement for its transgression.
Therefore none but The Messiah could redeem fallen man from
the curse or penalty of the broken law and bring him again into
harmony with it. The Messiah offered to take upon Himself
sinful man's guilt and shame in order to rescue him from
eternal ruin. He was willing to reach down to the very depths
of misery in order to do this. Heaven has made no other
provision whereby penitent man can be released from the
condemnation and thralldom of sin. This vicarious suffering of
a Substitute is clearly portrayed in Isaiah 53. If we would
familiarize ourselves with this scripture, there would open up
before us vistas of truth and avenues of research hitherto
undreamed of. We would gain a new conception of God's
character and would better understand His divine forbearance
and long-suffering with the sinner. The following is Isaiah's
description of the divine Substitute-the korban-which is the
Lamb of God: "Surely our infirmities He has borne, and carried

our sufferings: and we deemed Him one stricken, smitten of God, and afflicted. And He [was] wounded on account of our trangressions, He was bruised on account of our iniquities; the chastisement of our peace [was] upon Him, and by means of His stripes we have been healed. All of us have gone astray as sheep; each one to his own way, we have turned away our faces; and the LORD has caused the iniquity of all of us to fall on Him. He was oppressed, and was afflicted, and He opened not His mouth: He (was) brought as the lamb to the slaughter, and dumb as a sheep before its shearers, He opened not His mouth." Isaiah 53:4-7.

Who is meant by this "lamb" that is brought to the slaughter? Who is this Sufferer that turned away the sword of justice from the guilty sinner and permitted it to pierce His own heart? Of whom is it written that "The LORD has caused the iniquity of all of us to fall on Him"? None other than the blessed Messiah. [see chapter 5]. Seven centuries passed before the above prophecy recorded by Isaiah met its fulfillment. The long-looked-for Messiah then appeared. John "sees Yeshua coming toward him, and he says: Behold the Lamb of God, the One bearing the sin of the world." John 1: 29. Later "John stood, and two of his disciples, and looking at Yeshua walking, he said: Behold the Lamb of God." John 1:35,36. John, the forerunner of The Messiah, and also one of Israel's greatest prophets, introduced Yeshua as the Lamb of God. The ancient sacrificial lamb foreshadowed Him who was "the Lamb of God.

Paul, the Jewish apostle states: "The Messiah our Passover is sacrificed for us." 1 Corinthians 5:7. Yeshua was the true antitypical Paschal Lamb. Every major feature of the ancient paschal lamb had its counterpart and met its complete fulfillment in Yeshua the "Lamb of God." The Paschal lamb was set apart four days before it was slain. Yeshua's death was planned by leaders of the Sanhedrin several days before His crucifixion, and therefore He walked no more openly among the people. The Paschal lamb was to be without blemish. The Scripture declares of Yeshua that He was sinless. "The One [Yeshua] not knowing sin He [God] made to be sin in our behalf, in order that in Him we might be made the righteousness of God." 2 Corinthians 5: 21 (Gr.).

The Paschal lamb was killed the 14th day of Nisan "between the two evenings"or 3:00 to 4:00 o'clock in the afternoon. Yeshua was crucified the 14th day of Nisan and died in the ninth hour between 3:00 and 4:00 p.m., in the afternoon. Matthew 27:46,50; Luke 23:44-46. In order to save the first-born from certain death, it was not enough that the Paschal lamb be slain. The blood shed had to be sprinkled on the doorposts of the houses. In like manner, it is not sufficient to believe that The Messiah died for the world. We must believe that His blood was shed for us individually. Only as we ourselves appropriate the merits of that blood and apply the benefits of His atoning death to the soul-believing that God for The Messiah's sake forgives our sins and cleanses us from all iniquity-can we be shielded from the final destruction of sin and sinners. "But if we walk in the light as He [God] Himself is in the light, we have fellowship with each other, and the blood of Yeshua The Messiah, His Son, cleanses us from all sin." 1John 1:7. The flesh of the Passover lamb was to be eaten in the night, immediately following the sunset marking the close of the day on which it was slain. Yeshua died on the same day He was crucified. "And it was now about the sixth hour [noon], and darkness came over all the land until the ninth hour [about 3:00 p.m.],the sun failing [to shine]; and the veil of the Temple was rent in the midst. And crying with a great voice, Yeshua said: O Father, into Thy hands I commit My spirit. And saying this, He expired." Luke 23: 44-46 . The Paschal lamb was to be eaten with unleavened bread. In the Bible leaven is a type of sin. Unleavened bread, therefore, is symbolical of sincerity and truth. "Purge out ye the old leaven, in order that ye may be a new lump, as ye are unleavened. For, indeed, The Messiah our Passover [Lamb] was sacrificed for us. So let us not celebrate the festival with old leaven, nor with leaven of malice and evil; but with unleavened [bread] of sincerity and truth." 1Corinthians 5:7,8 . In like manner, the leaven of sin must be repented of and put away, and in sincerity and truth each of us must believe in The Messiah and receive life and nourishment from Him through His word. Not a bone of the Paschal lamb was to be broken. See Exodus 12:46; Numbers 9:12. The legs of the two thieves crucified with Yeshua were broken in order to hasten their death; but when the soldiers came to Yeshua, they found that He had already died. "The soldiers, therefore, came and they broke the legs of the first and of the other man having been crucified with Him (Yeshua:) and coming to Yeshua, when they saw Him already dead, they did not break His legs. For these things happened that the Scripture might be fulfilled: Not a bone of Him shall be broken." John 19:32,33,37. It is clear that the Paschal lamb was a symbol, a figure, an object lesson representing Yeshua, The Messiah, as the true Lamb of God. Thus we have given indisputable evidence that Yeshua is The Messiah, The Lamb of God. He died the very day and at the time of the day on which the Passover lamb was to be slain. The slaughter of the Paschal lamb brought Israel deliverance from physical bondage; the death of Yeshua,the Antitypical Lamb, delivers us from bondage to sin. Says God: " His own iniquities shall take the wicked himself, and he shall be holden with the cords of his sins." Proverbs 5:22 .

Sin enslaves a person. The sinner is held fast with the fetters of his own wicked habits. The deceiver, or adulterer, or liar may boast of his vaunted freedom, but in reality such a person is held in the worst kind of bondage; for he is a slave shackled by the chains of his own guilt and sinful habits. There is only one power that can break the dreadful hold that evil has upon the hearts of men, and that power is of God through The Messiah. He declares: "Verily, verily, I say unto you, Whosoever committeth sin is the servant of sin. If the Son therefore shall make you free, ye shall be free indeed." John 8:34,36. Only through the blood of Yeshua, the Lamb of God, can man resist and subdue the evil propensities of his fallen nature. Without this supernatural help, man is destined to go deeper into sin. "And sin, when it is finished, bringeth forth death." James 1:15. Yeshua says to all of us "If ye believe not that I am He [The Messiah], ye shall die in your sins." John 8:24.

Have you, dear reader, wandered far from God, feasting on the fruits of transgression, only to find yourself in bondage to sin? You seek to quiet a troubled conscience, with the thought that some day, perhaps in some terrible extremity, you will change your evil course. This, however, is not so easily done. Every sinful indulgence strengthens the soul's aversion to God. The man who manifests an infidel hardihood, or a stolid indifference to divine truth, is but reaping the harvest of what he has sown. In all the Bible there is not a more fearful warning set forth against trifling with evil than may be found in the words of the wise man, that the sinner "shall be holden with the cords of sin." Proverbs 5:22 . The Holy Scriptures assure us: "And God commends His own love toward us, because that while we were yet sinners, The Messiah died in our behalf." Romans 5:8.

The Messiah would never have had to die for us if man had never broken the law, if man had never sinned. But when man sinned, the law demanded the death penalty. God prepared a way that man need not die or perish eternally; The Messiah died in man's stead. He gave His life for mankind. And remember: "God commends His own love toward us because that while we were yet sinners, The Messiah died in our behalf." Romans 5:8.

To illustrate the debt of gratitude we owe to our divine Deliverer, the blessed Messiah, and so we may understand Romans 5:8 a little more clearly, note the following story: A little boy was playing outside his home with a ball, while his mother was sitting on the porch knitting. He was just a little fellow four years old. He would throw the ball against the building, and as it bounced back, he would catch it. But once it went over his head and out into the street, so he rushed out after it without looking, and an automobile struck him. His mother screamed and ran to the street. There was the child lie in a pool of blood. They rushed him to the hospital; the father was notified, and soon joined them. The doctor said to the father and mother: "Your child has a 50-50 chance of living. However, he has lost much blood because of hemorrhages. There is only one way to save his life, and that is by blood transfusion." So they tested the father's blood, but found they could not use it because it was not of right type. The mother, however, had the same rare type of blood as the child. So they took a pint of blood from her and administered it to the child.

A few days later the doctor called at the home of the father and mother and said: "Your child is beginning to fail again. I fear he will die unless we can obtain the proper type of blood, and we hope someone will volunteer it." No one came who had the needed rare type blood, so the mother pleaded with the doctor to take another pint of her blood. Said the doctor, "You are not strong enough. She said, "Take my blood; let my child live." He said, "I will take another pint if you will promise me to go to bed for a week."

A few days later the doctor returned and said to the father and mother: "Your son is failing again. I fear there is nothing we can do. We have advertised for blood, but of hundreds of people who came, not one of them had the right type. Please do not ask me to take any more blood from you. I might go to jail if I do." The mother arose and kneeled at the doctor's feet and pleaded with him to take whatever blood might be necessary. He said, "I ought not to do it, but I will take a half a pint." Again the child rallied. A few days later the doctor came to the home, and the mother was still in bed. This time the doctor said to them: "Now I am afraid I have bad news. Your child is failing again. I cannot take any more of your blood, no matter how badly you want me to nor how earnestly you plead with me, for if I take another pint of your blood you will die. But I have notified those in charge of the laboratory at the hospital that the first individual who comes with that type of blood, they are to take the blood and administer it to the child."

The next morning the husband went to work. After he had left the house, the mother arose and dressed and phoned for a taxicab. She said to the taxicab driver, "Take me to the nearest barber shop." As she stepped out of the taxicab, she said, "You wait for me." She went inside and said to the barber, "Give me a man's haircut." This done, she went out and stepped in the taxicab and went back home. Arriving at home, she hastened into her husband's wardrobe and dressed herself in her husband's suit and shoes and hat. Then she called another taxicab and told him to take her to the hospital where her little boy was dying. Arriving there she took her place in line with the people who were waiting to have their blood tested. One of the interns came over and took a specimen of her blood, examined it, and took it to the doctor in charge, saying, "Doctor, I have a man out there with the rare type of blood which we need." He said, "Well, quickly take a pint of his blood and give it to the child." She dearly loved him. Finally, after the intern had administered the blood transfusion, he came back and a nurse said, "Did you hear about that man who fell unconscious? He is in a coma now." He said, "Where is he?" She replied, "In that room over there." He went in and said, "Undress the man and put him to bed." But when they went to undress the man, they found that it was a woman. Suspecting she might be the mother of the child, they called the doctor who had charge of the case. When he entered the room, he said, "It is the mother, she will die."

Going to the boy's room, he found instead of the child lying in his bed too weak to move, he was standing, holding to the crib, and saying, "I want my mamma, I want my mamma." He said then, "Sonny, you will live, but your mother will die." He called for the father, and the doctor told the husband what had happened. He said to the intern, "I want you to administer a stimulant to this mother in order that she may see her child alive before she dies." The stimulant was administered, and soon the mother began to rally and opened her eyes. The first thing she caught sight of was her little boy, whom the father was holding, and she said faintly, "Sonny,Sonny." The doctor said, "Yes, Sonny will live. He has passed the crises." She looked at her boy and said, "Thank God," and laid back her head and died

As that mother gave her blood that her son might live, so Yeshua, The Messiah, gave His blood that we might live. Isn't it time now to give your heart to Yeshua surrender all to Him, that when The Messiah comes again you may be saved.

CHAPTER 9

Jesus The Jew!
Were His Teachings Jewish?

DURING the last decades there has been an amazing change in the attitude of our Jewish people toward Jesus. To illustrate how far reaching and significant this change in sentiment has been is, perhaps, best expressed by the following statement which points out that "a great historic movement of the character and importance of Christianity can not have arisen without a great personality to call it into existence and to give it shape and direction. Jesus of Nazareth had a mission from God (see Maimonides,'Yad,' Melakim,xi 4, and the other passages quoted in **JEWISH ENCYCLOPEDIA iv.56 et seq., s.v. CHRISTIANITY);** and he must have had the spiritual power and fitness to be chosen for it." —**The Jewish Encyclopedia,** volume 7, p. 167, column 1, article "Jesus of Nazareth."

Dr. Stephen S. Wise, Rabbi of the Free Synagogue of New York, delivered a sensational lecture in Carnegie Hall on December 20, 1925, his subject being "A Jew's Views of Jesus." In it, he announced that he read the book **Jesus of Nazareth,** by Dr. Joseph Klausner, professor of the Hebrew University in Jerusalem, who, after diligent research, advised all other Jews to accept the fact of the existence of Jesus. And Dr. Wise added: "For years I have been led to believe,like thousands of other Jews, that Jesus never existed. 'Jesus was a myth' is the common belief among many Jews. I say this is not so. Jesus was." —Quoted in **The New York Times,** December 21,1925, p.24.

Not so many years ago, there were skeptics who questioned whether Jesus ever existed as an actual human being. They suggested that He was merely a figment of the imagination, a legendary person, a myth. But where are these doubters today? They are so rare as to be practically nonexistent. Why is this? The answer is that scientific research and exhaustive, unbiased study have forever settled this question. No scholarly person today doubts that Jesus existed. Dr. Joseph Klausner, after giving many years of careful and scholarly research to the question of the historical existence of Jesus, has shown "it is unreasonable to question either the existence of Jesus (as certain scholars have done both in the eighteenth century and in our own time) or his general character as it is depicted in these Gospels. This is the single historical value which we can attribute to the early Talmudical accounts of Jesus."-**Jesus of Nazareth,** p.20, Beacon Press. He cites not only Josephus **Jewish Antiquities,** Book 18, chapter 3, section 3, the Jewish historian; and Tacitus **Annals,** book 15, chapter 44, and Suetonius **Lives of the Ceasars,** "Claudius," chapter 25, both Roman historians; but also the **Babylonian Talmud,** as bearing witness to the fact that Jesus was a Jew and that he lived and died in Palestine. The Talmudic affirmation clearly states: "On the eve of the Passover Yesu was hanged. But since nothing was brought forth in his favor he was hanged on the eve of the Passover."-**Sanhedrin** 43a, volume 1, p. 281, Soncino Press. Editorial footnote 6 on the same page states that the text in one manuscript says "Yesu the Nazarean," while footnote 7 says that a Florentine manuscript adds to the time, "and on the eve of the Sabbath."

The most amazing evidence by far that Jesus was a real historical being, and not some legendary figure, is the amazing narrative of His life found in the four Gospels. From this faithful record we learn that Jesus lived only to bless others and to bring light, hope, and cheer into their lives. Jesus died at the early age of 33, and yet, He has influenced the course of history infinitely more than all the great men, kings, emperors, rulers, potentates, statesmen, philosophers, inventors, and famed scientists put together! One of the most amazing facts of history is that Jesus, a Jew, split the centuries in two. Everything before Him is dated B.C.E. (or B.C.), and everything after Him is dated C.E. (or A.D.). All history revolves about Him. Nevertheless, it has the same meaning. If so great a personality as Jesus could split the centuries in two, a fact which the entire world today follows, then He really warrants our investigation. Great men have come and gone, but Jesus, the Jew, transcends them all. It is not the 20th century after Çaesar, but it is the 20th century after Jesus. The greatest of men are but pigmies in comparison with Jesus.

As Jews, we want the facts. If so great a figure as Jesus was a Jew, and if His teachings were Jewish, then we should claim Him as our own Jewish brother and not let the Gentiles have all the glory. Because of the incomparable greatness of Jesus, some have presumed to question the Jewish origin of Jesus. Some have even asserted that He was a Gentile of

Galilee. None, however, need to be disturbed by such an absurd and fantastic invention. We have unimpeachable evidence of the Jewish genealogical records.

Up to the time of the destruction of the Temple in 70 C.E., every Hebrew male child, especially the first-born, was registered in the Temple archives. Thus, an unbroken genealogical record was kept. One reason why this was done was to help identify the true Messiah, whose coming had been anticipated and looked forward to by the Jewish nation. Many a pious mother in Israel fondly hoped that she might be the one chosen to give birth to the long-looked-for Redeemer of mankind. According to these genealogical records, Jesus was a direct descendant of David. We read: " The book of the generation of Yeshua The Messiah, the Son of David." Matthew 1:1. Jesus was often addressed and appealed to as the Son of David. We quote a few texts: "And when Jesus departed thence, two blind men followed Him, crying, and saying, Thou Son of David, have mercy on us." Matthew 9:27.

"And, behold, a woman of Canaan came out of the same coasts, and cried unto Him, saying, Have mercy on me, O Lord, Thou Son of David; my daughter is grievously vexed with a devil." Matthew 15:22. "And they came to Jericho: and as He went out of Jericho with His disciples and a great number of people, blind Bartimaeus, the son of Timaeus, sat by the highway side begging. And when he heard that it was Jesus of Nazareth, he began to cry out, and say, Jesus, Thou Son of David, have mercy on me." Mark 10:46,47. "Then was brought unto Him one possessed with a devil, blind, and dumb: and He healed him, insomuch that the blind and dumb both spake and saw. And all the people were amazed, and said, Is not this the Son of David?" Matthew 12:22,23. "And the multitudes that went before, and that followed, cried, saying, Hosanna to the Son of David: Blessed is He that cometh in the name of the Lord; Hosanna in the highest." Matthew 21:9.

In His day, and for the above stated reasons, no one ever thought of challenging His right to the title "the Son of David." The very features of His countenance and the manner of His dress bore eloquent testimony of His Jewish origin. This explains why the Samaritan woman who talked with Jesus at Jacob's well knew that He was a Jew. "How is it," she asked, "that Thou, being a Jew askest drink of me, which am a woman of Samaria?" John 4:9. In Luke 2:21 we have the record that when Jesus was eight days old, He was circumcised in

harmony with the instruction laid down in the book of Moses.
We quote: "And when eight days were accomplished for the
circumcising of the child, His name was called JESUS
[Yeshua]." It is written that when He reached the Bar Mitzvah
age,.."When He was twelve years old, they went up to
Jerusalem after the custom of the feast." Luke 2:42. After He
began His public ministry at the age 30, He was known as
"Rabbi." We read in John 3:2 that Nicodemus, a ruler of Jews
and an honored member of the Jewish Sanhedrin,addressed
Him thus during a night interview:"Rabbi, we know that Thou
art a teacher come from God."

To maintain Jesus was anything else but a Jew is contrary
to historical evidence. His Jewish ancestry cannot be
successfully disputed, and Jews can take justifiable pride in
that fact. Joseph Klausner, well known Jewish author, says: "It
is, therefore, manifest that Jesus was a true Jew of Jewish
family, for Galilee was, in His time, mainly populated by Jews;
while there could be no stronger proof of His Jewishness than
His essentially Jewish character and manner of life." -**Jesus of
Nazareth,** p.233.

Were the teachings that Jesus propounded Jewish? Were
His instructions and doctrine in harmony with those recorded in
the Bible by the Jewish prophets of old? For, in the last
analysis, the Bible, the Word of the living God, must be the
criterion, the standard, by which we should judge all religious
doctrine. A genuine teacher of truth must be guided by the
Holy Scriptures. Were he to add or take away aught from the
Sacred Canon, he would no longer merit the confidence of the
people. We are admonished in the Torah by Moses the
prophet: "Ye shall not add unto the word which I command
you, neither shall ye diminish ought from it, that ye may keep
the commandments of the Lord your God which I command
you." Deuteronomy 4:21. The prophet Isaiah counsels us thus
"To the law and to the testimony: If they speak not according
to this word, then there is for one no dawning light." Isaiah
8:20.

One of the fundamental teachings of Moses is the unity of
God, or monotheism, in contrast with the system of multiple
gods, or polytheism, of the heathen. No Scripture is perhaps
more frequently quoted by the Jews than the "Shema" in
Deuteronomy 6:4 , "Hear, O Israel: the LORD our God is one
LORD." Did Jesus reaffirm this teachings? In the historical
record it is stated: "And Jesus answered him, The first of all

commandments, is, Hear, O Israel; The Lord our God is one Lord." Mark 12:29.

Above any other truth, Moses and the Prophets emphasized and re-emphasized the immutability of God's law of Ten Commandments. How did Jesus relate Himself to the eternal, unchangeable law of God? In Matthew 5:17,18 He said: "Think not that I am come to destroy the law, or the prophets: I am not come to destroy, but to fulfill. For verily I say unto you, Till heaven and earth pass, one jot or one tittle shall in no wise pass from the law, till all be fulfilled."

According to the teaching of Jesus not even a "jot" or "tittle" of the law can ever be abrogated or cancelled. The "jot" refers to the yod- the smallest letter of the Hebrew alphabet; while the "tittle" is the extra flourish which the scribes gave to certain letters in copying the Holy Writings. Jesus made this statement in order to show the people how He regarded God's law as compared with tradition. Here is the way Jewish tradition has regarded it: "Three (classes of persons) are to be called deniers of the Torah: (1). He who maintains that the Torah is not of divine origin, or who only thinks that a verse or a word thereof has been declared by Moses himself (without divine verbal inspiration), (2) has already then denied the integrity of the Torah. (3). He who maintains that God has substituted (or exchanged) one law (or statute) for another. Each of these opinions is to be considered (or regarded) as a denial of the Torah."- Maimonides (Moses ben Maimon), **Yad Ha-Hazakah,** chap.3,par.8 of Hilkoth Teshuvah; Bernard S. Jacobson's translation pp.18, 19.

The Rabbis say that not one commandment, yea, not "even one verse or one word" can be deleted; while Jesus taught that not even the smallest letter of the law can under any circumstances be expunged. Which of the two would you say was more zealous, more ardent in teaching the immutability of the law of God? The prophet Isaiah speaking of this phase of The Messiah's work says: "The LORD is well pleased for His [The Messiah's] righteousness' sake; He will magnify the law, and make it honorable." Isaiah 42:21.

How did Jesus magnify the law and make it honorable? Below are a few questions which are answered from the New Testament concerning the teachings of Jesus:

1. Q. Did Jesus keep the Sabbath as was the custom and religion of the Jewish people of His day?

A. "He came to Nazareth, where He had been brought up: and, as His custom was, He went into the synagogue on the Sabbath day, and stood up for to read." Luke 4:16.

2. Q. What did Jesus teach His followers concerning the Sabbath?

A. "But pray ye that your flight be not in the winter, neither on the Sabbath day." Matthew 24:20.

3. Q. Whom did Jesus say would have a right to the tree of life?

A. "Blessed are they that do His (God's) command-ments, that they may have right to the tree of life, and may enter in through the gates into the city." Revelation 22:14.

4. Q. What did Jesus answer when He was asked, "Good Master, what good thing shall I do, that I may have eternal life?" Matthew 19:16.

A. "If thou wilt enter into life, keep the command-ments." Matthew 19:17.

Jesus came to this world in order to minister to every need of humanity. No building in Israel was large enough to hold the multitudes that thronged to hear Him. His life was one of constant self-sacrifice. He had no home of His own. He said: "The foxes have holes, and the birds of the air have nests; but the Son of man hath not where to lay His head." Matthew 8:20. Though poor, He made many rich. He recognized no distinction of nationality, rank, or creed. To Him, Jew and Gentile, rich and poor, were linked in a common brotherhood and were equal before God. He passed no human being by as worthless. He helped all who were in sorrow and affliction. He lifted up those who were bowed down and comforted the hopeless and distressed. Like a vital current, He diffused life and joy wherever He went. No cry from a soul in need went unheeded.

Think of the Jewish woman who had an issue of blood for twelve years and who was healed the same instant that she touched Jesus' garment! Mark 5:25-29. Then think of the man born blind whose sight Jesus restored! John, chapter 9. Think of the leper whom Jesus instantaneously and miraculously healed! Matthew 8:2,3. And what shall we say of the blind and dumb man who was possessed by a demon and whom Jesus healed, "insomuch that the blind and dumb (man) both spake and saw." Matthew 12:22. Is it any wonder that the Jewish people of those days loved this great Healer and Benefactor? He toiled daily, teaching, healing the sick, giving sight to the blind. Not one who sought His help was turned away. Jewish mothers, with their sick and dying babes, pressed through surging throngs in order to come within the reach of His notice. At His touch the disease fled. To all alike, Jesus dispensed His life-giving power, and all gave praise and honor to Him who had done such great and wonderful things for them. Why should they not love and adore Him?

Spies were sent on His track to listen to His words in order to find some occasion against Him, but even they had to confess: "Never man spake like this Man." John 7:46. Their hard hearts melted as they listened to His truth-filled words so full of heavenly love and compassion. Their testimony was indeed true. And the reason why Jesus spoke as no other man ever spoke was because He lived as no other man ever lived. It is equally true that He died as no other man ever died. He bore, without a murmur, the bloody scourging of the Roman soldiers; He silently endured the infamous abuse of wicked men and finally fainted from sheer exhaustion while carrying the Roman cross to the place of execution. No complaint came from His lips as the Roman soldiers drove the nails through His tender flesh, but instead He uttered this prayer for His enemies: "Father, forgive them; for they know not what they do." Luke 23:34.

His last moments of agony were filled with deeds of benevolence. When the dying penitent thief addressed Jesus as He hung upon the cross, with the blood drops flowing from His head, His hands and feet, he pleaded: "Lord, remember me when Thou comest into the Kingdom." Luke 23:42. Quickly the answer came, so full of assurance, compassion, and love: "Thou shalt be with Me in paradise." Luke 23:43. He also remembered His widowed mother in His dying hour. Looking down into her grief-stricken face and then upon John, one of His most faithful and devoted disciples, He said: "Woman, behold thy son!" Then He said to John: "Behold thy mother." John 19:26,27. John understood Jesus' words, accepted the sacred trust, and from that hour took her into his home and tenderly cared for her the rest of her life.

What submission and resignation were His as in His last dying moments He uttered the words: "Father, into Thy hands I commend My spirit." Luke 23:46. A noted Jewish historian has said of Jesus' death: "He was the only man born of whom it may be said without exaggeration that he accomplished more in his death than in his life; Golgotha became another Sinai to the historic world."-Heinrich Graetz, **History of the Jews**, volume 2,p.91, Hebrew Publishing Company.

To list all the eulogies of Jesus uttered by leading Jews would fill many volumes. We must, therefore, limit ourselves to just a few testimonies:

Dr. David Philipson, Rabbi of Mound Street Temple in Cincinnati, Ohio, and professor at Hebrew Union College: "There is no backwardness nor hesitancy on the part of modern Jewish thought in acknowledging the greatness of the teacher of Nazareth, the sweetness of his character, the power of his genius." Quoted by George Croly, **Tarry Thou Till I Come**, p.566 , Grossett and Dunlap.

Dr. Max (Simon) Nordau, noted Jewish litterateur and philosopher in Europe, and Theodore Herzl's associate in the leadership of the Zionist Movement, declared: "Jesus is our soul, as he is flesh of our flesh. Who, then, could think of excluding him from the people of Israel? Every time that a Jew mounted to the sources and contemplated Christ alone, without his pretended faithful, he cried, with tenderness and admiration. Putting aside the Messianic mission, this man is ours. He honors our race and we claim him as we claim the Gospels-flowers of Jewish literature and only Jewish." Quoted by George Croly, **Ibid.**, p. 559.

Dr. Kaufmann Kohler, famous Rabbi of Temple Beth-El in New York and president of Hebrew Union College, whom Dr.Isidor Singer, founder and editor of **The Jewish Encyclopedia**, called "the greatest living Jewish theologian of America," stated: "Jesus, the living man, was the teacher and practicer of the tenderest love for God and man, the paragon of piety, humility, and self-surrender; He was one of the best and truest sons of the Synagogue. Did he not say, 'I have not come to destroy the law, but to fulfill it'? He had nothing of the rigidity of the schoolman, none of the pride of the philosopher and recluse, nor even the implacable zeal of the ancient prophet to excite the popular wrath; he came only to weep with the sorrowing, to lift up the downtrodden, to save and to heal."-As quoted by Isidor Singer, **A Religion of Truth, Justice, and Peace,** p.117, The Amos Society, New York City.

Dr. Joseph Klausner has told us also: "Like a real Jew, Jesus regards the prayers of the heathen as 'vain repetition,' 'babbling.' He therefore composed this brief prayer: 'Our Father which art in heaven, Hallowed be Thy name, Thy kingdom come. Thy will be done, as in heaven, so on earth. Give us this day our daily bread and forgive us our debts as we also have forgiven our debtors. And bring us not into temptation, but deliver us from evil one' (Matthew 6:9-12). It is a remarkable prayer, universal in its appeal, earnest, brief and full of devotion. Every single clause in it is, however, to be found in Jewish prayers and sayings in the Talmud."-**Jesus of Nazareth,** pp.386, 387.

In his lecture "The Gospel as a Document of History," Dr. Leo Baeck, one of modern Judaism's most noted scholars, has given us this picture of Jesus: "In the old Gospel which is thus opened up before us, we encounter a man with noble features who lived in the land of the Jews in tense and excited times and helped and labored and suffered and died: a man out of the Jewish people who walked on Jewish paths with Jewish faith and hopes. His spirit was at home in the Holy Scriptures, and his imagination and thought were anchored there; and he proclaimed and taught the Word of God because God had given it to him to hear and to preach. We are confronted by a man who won his disciples among his people: men who had been looking for The Messiah, the son of David, who had been promised; In this old tradition we behold a man who is Jewish in every feature and trait of his character, manifesting in every particular what is pure and good in Judaism. This man could have developed as he came to be only on the soil of Judaism; and only on this soil, too, could he find his disciples and followers as they were. Here alone, in this Jewish sphere, in this Jewish atmosphere of trust and longing, could this man live his life and meet his death- a Jew among Jews. Jewish history and Jewish reflection may not pass him by nor ignore him. Since he was, no time has been without him; nor has there been a time which was not challenged by the epoch that would consider him its starting point. When this old tradition confronts us in this manner, then the Gospel, which was originally something Jewish, becomes a book-and certainly not

a minor work-within Jewish literature. This is not because, or
not only because, it contains sentences which also appear in the
same or a similar form in the Jewish works of that time. Nor is
it such-in fact, it is even less so- because the Hebrew or
Aramaic breaks again and again through the word forms and
sentence formations of the Greek translation. Rather it is a
Jewish book because-by all means and entirely because-the
pure air of which it is full and which it breathes is that of the
Holy Scriptures; because a Jewish spirit, and none other, lives
in it; because Jewish faith and Jewish hope, Jewish suffering
and Jewish distress,Jewish knowledge and Jewish expectations,
and these alone, resound through it- a Jewish book in the midst
of Jewish books. Judaism may not pass it by, nor mistake it,
nor wish to give up all claims here. Here, too, Judaism should
comprehend and take note of what is its own."-**Judaism and
Christianity**,pp. 100-102, The World Publishing Company.

What should be our relation, as Jews, to Jesus? It is not
enough to agree that He was Jewish and that His teachings are
in accord with that of our prophets. In the light of the
unparalleled nobility and uprightness of His character, it is our
bounden duty and our God-given privilege to investigate Jesus.
Let us, therefore, lay aside all preconceived ideas and put away
all prejudices. Jesus was born, lived, and died a Jew. He is our
Jewish brother.

CHAPTER 10

The Old and New Testaments– Do They Agree?

EARLY in king Rehoboam's reign (931-913 B.C.E.), 10 tribes of Israel revolted in protest against high taxes and established themselves as the separate "kingdom of Israel" under the rule of Jeroboam I in the northern part of the Holy Land. Rehoboam was thereafter the ruler of the "Kingdom of Judah," which consisted mainly of the tribes of Benjamin and Judah with Jerusalem as its capital. This great breach in Israelite unity was never healed. The Northern kingdom was destroyed by the Assyrians in 722 B.C.E. and the Southern by the Babylonians in 586 B.C.E. Almost all of the survivors of both were dispersed by their conquerors into distant heathen lands.

Under a decree in 536 B.C.E., issued by Cyrus the Great, king of Persia, about 50,000 Jewish exiles returned with Zerubbabel to Jerusalem and restored the Jewish commonwealth. It grew in strength and maintained a precarious existence in spite of tremendous difficulties during the world dominion of the Persians and the Greeks. In 63 B.C.E. it was incorporated by armies into the Roman empire. But the number of Jews who continued to live in heathen lands often equaled or exceeded the Jewish population of the Judean commonwealth. And as a result of the Babylonian Captivity, Aramaic largely replaced Hebrew as the common language in Jewish life. Our people in Gentile lands were constantly exposed to the pernicious influence of the heathenism surrounding them. They could not read the Holy Scriptures in Hebrew, and were isolated by distance from regular attendance and religious instruction at the Temple services and the celebration of the yearly festivals in Jerusalem. Our Jewish leaders became deeply concerned for the spiritual welfare of our people. As a result, synagogues were built for Jewish communities in many places throughout the world in order that they might regularly worship the God of Israel on the Sabbath day and be instructed in the Holy Scriptures. Religious literature was provided at an early date in the form of Targums. This consisted of paraphrases and interpretative translations of the Holy Scriptures from Hebrew into Aramaic. As Hellenic culture became dominant in the Graeco-Roman world, Greek became the most widely used language, especially in the European, Asian, and African countries near the Mediterranean Sea. For example, the city of Alexandria in Egypt was founded by and named for Alexander the Great in 332 B.C.E., as the conqueror of that country. Many Jews were present on that occasion. In fact, the one million Jews resided in Egypt early in the first century C.E. as reported by one of its official spokesmen. Alexandria alone has been estimated to be 200,000 at that time.

Ptolemy 1 (Soter), a leading general of Alexander the Great, made himself king of Egypt and thereby founded the Ptolemaic dynasty of Greek-speaking monarchs who reigned there till the country was annexed to the Roman empire in 30 B.C.E. With the favor and encouragement of his son, Ptolemy ll (Philadelpus), king of Egypt (287-247 B.C.E.,) Jewish scholars began to translate the entire text of the Hebrew Scriptures into Greek since this was the most universally used language of that age. Yeshua ben Sira (Sirach), a Jewish teacher of religion and ethics, has reported that when he was in Egypt in 132 B.C.E., he found that "the law, and the prophets, and the other books of our fathers," were already currently in use among the people there.

The Jewish writers, who penned the New Testament Scriptures in the first century C.E. wrote them in Greek, so they might be read by the most people. Later both the Old and the New Testament Scriptures were translated into other major languages of the world. In fact, the demand for the Holy Scriptures in Greek became so important the Jewish sages arranged for new Greek translations of the Hebrew text to be made. One such version was that of Aquila, a proselyte, in the reign of Roman Emperor Hadrian (117-138 C.E.). Another was prepared by Theodotion, also a proselyte, prior to 182 C.E. His Greek translation of the Book of Daniel became very popular. The Jews who wrote the New Testament Scriptures followed the precedent (already set by our Jewish sages who initiated the translation of the Hebrew Scriptures into Greek in the third century B.C.E.) by transliterating the Hebrew words **Yehoshua'** (**Yeshua'** in Aramaic) and **Mashiach** as **'Iesous** and **Messias** respectively in Greek. Thus, the terms "Jesus" and "Messiah" (meaning "Anointed One") in our English versions of the New Testament Scriptures are transliterations bequeathed to us by our ancient and scholarly Jewish translators of the Bible. In fact, in 36 out of the 39 instances, our ancient Jewish scholars rendered the Hebrew noun **Mashiach** as **Christos** ("Anointed One") when they prepared the Greek version. Especially significant is the additional fact they rendered **Mashiach** as **Christos** in the Messianic prophecy of Daniel 9:24-27 in both the Septuagint and the Theodotion versions. The New Testament writers, therefore, merely followed this Jewish precedent of using the Greek noun **Christos** as the correct equivalent of **Mashiach** in Hebrew.

Julius Caesar wrote his **Gallic War** between 58 and 50 B.C.E., but the oldest manuscript of it now known to exist is one penned about 900 years after he wrote. Livy's **Roman History** originally comprised 142 books, but only 35 of them have survived. That work was composed between 59 B.C.E. and 17 C.E.. Only one manuscript of it, consisting of portions of books three to six, dates back as far as the fourth century C.E. The **Histories**, written by Tacitus 100 C.E., consisted of 14 books, but only four and a half of these have survived. Of the 16 books of his **Annals**, only 10 survive in full and two in part. The text of those two works now depend entirely on two old manuscripts, one of the ninth century and the other of the eleventh century.

The **History** by Thucydides (460-400 B.C.E.) survives in eight manuscripts, the earliest of which belongs to about 900 C.E., plus a few scraps of papyrus from the beginning of the Common Era. The same can be said of the **History** by Herodotus. But there exist about 4,000 manuscripts of the New Testament in whole or in part. See F.F. Bruce, **The New Testament Documents: Are They Reliable?** pp.14-20, W.B. Eerdmans Publishing Company. C.C.McCown's article "The Earliest Christian Books" in **The Biblical Archeologist Reader,** pp. 251-261, Anchor Books. A first-century date for the New Testament writings has been reasonably established. The evidence for it is much greater than for many of the writings of classical Greek and Roman works, the authenticity of which is not questioned. Some papyrus fragments have been found which papyrological experts have dated as not later than 150 C.E. Earlier still, is a papyrus fragment containing John 8:31,33 which is dated as about 130 C.E.. This date is within 40 years of the death of John. This papyrus document found in

1917 is now in the John Rylands Library in Manchester, England. Historical evidence reveals John wrote his Gospel shortly before his death at Ephesus near the end of the first century.

Dr. Joseph Klausner, a Jewish scholar noted for his historical research on the life of Jesus of Nazareth, writes; "If we had ancient sources like those in the Gospels for the history of Alexander the Great or Julius Caesar for example, we should not cast any doubt upon them whatsoever. It is true that the Evangelists were influenced by religious views and religious propaganda; but do the political views and political propaganda by which ancient historians were influenced, consciously or unconsciously render invalid or blur historical data any less than do religious opinions and inclinations? If skeptical and hairsplitting criticism like this were applied to the historical sources for the life and views of Charlemagne or Mohammed, we should not have left of them anything of even relative historical validity except their mere existence."-**From Jesus to Paul,** p. 260, Beacon Press.

The New Testament Greek is not the classical kind, but the Greek of the common people of the first century C.E. However, in one respect it is noticeably distinctive, and that is the abundance of words, phrases, and thoughts derived from the Hebrew Scripture. The variety of Hebrew words, constructions, and phrases occurring in the Greek text of the New Testament reveal the pious men who wrote it were truly Jews devout in heart and mind. If all the copies of the Old Testament were suddenly to vanish from the world, it would be possible to recover much of it by culling out all the Old Testament quotations and references found in the New! The New Testament contains about 200 direct quotations from the Old, numerous loose quotations, and a large number of indirect quotations and allusions to the Old Testament. The following list gives the number of direct quotations from the various Old Testament books contained in the New Testament:

Genesis .... 28 times	Hosea .... 8 times
Joel .... 2 times	Amos .... 2 times
Jonah .... 1 time	Micah .... 2 times
Habakkuk .... 3 times	Haggai .... 1 time
Zechariah .... 7 times	Malachi .... 3 times
Ezekiel .... 2 times	Daniel .... 3 times
Exodus .... 29 times	Leviticus .... 8 times
Numbers .... 5 times	Deuteronomy .... 28 times
I & II Samuel ... 3 times	I & II Kings .... 4 times
Job .... 3 times	Psalms .... 73 times
Proverbs .... 11 times	Isaiah .... 77 times
Jeremiah .... 7 times	

Both Testaments are linked in a close and sacred partnership without one discordant note between them. The two espouse the same cause of truth and righteousness. Indeed, the New Testament not only reaffirms the truths taught in the Old but emphasizes and magnifies their importance. Let us enumerate some of the basic Old Testament teachings which are proclaimed and glorified in the New:

a. The Old Testament teaches God created the world in six literal days and rested on the seventh day. Genesis 2:1-3. This fundamental Scriptural truth is reaffirmed in the New Testament:

"The works (of creation) were finished from the foundation of the world. For He (God) spake in a certain place of the seventh day on this wise, And God did rest the seventh day from all His works." Hebrews 4:3,4.

b. Sabbath observance is of perpetual obligation. Exodus 31:16,17. This duty has not been nullified or repealed in the New Testament, but rather confirmed

"Pray ye that your flight (from Judea during the invasion by the Roman armies) be not in the winter, neither on the sabbath day." Matthew 24:20.

c. The creation of Adam and Eve, as described in the Torah, is reaffirmed in the New Testament as follows:

"Have ye not read (in the Torah) that He which made them at the beginning made them male and female?" Matthew 19:4.

d. Sin entered into the world through one man-Adam. This fact is reasserted:

"By one man (Adam) sin entered into the world, and death by sin; and so death passed upon all men, for that all have sinned." Romans 5:12.

e. In Abraham all the families of the earth were to be blessed. Genesis 12: 1-3; 22:18. This is reiterated:

"In thee shall all nations be blessed. So then they which be of faith are blessed with faithful Abraham." Galatians 3:8,9.

f. God entrusted ancient Israel with the truths essential for the salvation of all mankind. Exodus 19:5,6. This important fact is also emphasized.

"Salvation is of the Jews" (John 4:22), "who are Israelites; to whom pertaineth the adoption, and the glory, and the covenants, and the giving of the law and the service of God, and the promises." (Romans 9:4).

The New Testament regards the entiree Old Testament, from Moses to Malachi, as divinely inspired and teaches that faith in it as God's Word is one of the conditions of salvation: "If they hear not Moses and the prophets, neither will they be persuaded, though one rose from the dead." Luke 16:31.

One of the most important Old Testament predictions is God's promise to make a new covenant with His people. "Behold, the days come, saith the LORD, that I will make a new covenant with the house of Israel, and with the house of Judah: not according to the convenant that I made with their fathers in the day that I took them by the hand to bring them out of the land of Egypt; which my covenant they brake, although I was a lord over them, saith the LORD: But this shall be the covenant that I will make with the house of Israel; After those days, saith the LORD, I will put my law in their inward parts, and write it in their hearts; and will be their God, and they shall be my people." Jeremiah 31:31-33 . The reader will note the promise was made, not to the Gentiles, but _**to the house of Israel and to the house of Judah.**_ Has God failed to make this new covenant which He promised to both houses of Israel? impossible! The God of Israel is a covenant-keeping God. "Hath He said, and shall He not do it ? or hath He spoken, and shall He not make it good?" Numbers 23:19 (H). That the above prophecy of Jeremiah is fulfilled by the New

Testament writings is admitted by many Jewish thinkers. The following quotation from **The Jewish Encyclopedia,** volume 9,p. 246, is very much to the point: "The name of 'New Testament' was given to the gospels and to other apostolic writings, inasmuch as they were composed with the purpose of showing that the Messianic prophecies had been fulfilled and a new covenant or dispensation had taken place. The idea of the new covenant is based chiefly upon Jeremiah 31:31-34."

The very existence of such a book as the New Testament, is a living testimony that God has remembered His promise of a New Covenant which He made to His people. An important prophecy predicting the outpouring of the **Ruach ha-Koodesh**—God's Holy Spirit—upon His people is recorded in the book of Joel. "And it shall come to pass afterward, that I will pour out My Spirit upon all flesh; and your sons and your daughters shall prophesy, your old men shall dream dreams, your young men shall see visions." "And it shall come to pass, that whosoever shall call on the name of the LORD shall be delivered." Joel 3:1,5.

Joel wrote his book in the eighth century B.C.E.. NO record in the writings of the Old Testament Prophets (who lived contemporaneously with the Prophet Joel, or subsequent to the time when this prediction was made) that this remarkable prediction was ever fulfilled. When, then, was God's Holy Spirit poured out upon His people? "When the day of Pentecost **(Hag Shabu'oth)** had come, they were all together in one place. And suddenly a sound came from heaven like the rush of mighty wind, and it filled all the house where they were sitting. And they were all filled with the Holy Spirit and began to speak in other tongues, as the Spirit gave them utterance. Now there were dwelling in Jerusalem Jews, devout men from every nation under heaven. And at this sound the multitude came together, and they were bewildered,because each one heard them speaking in his own language. And they were amazed and wondered, saying, 'Are not all these who are speaking Galileans? And how is it that we hear, each of us in his own native language?' But Peter, standing with the eleven, lifted up his voice and addressed them, 'Men of Judea and all who dwell in Jerusalem, let this be known to you, and give ear to my words. For these men are not drunk, as you suppose, since it is only the third hour of the day; but this is what was spoken by the prophet Joel.'" Acts 2:1-16. This prophecy and its fulfillment is one of many examples of the interdependence of the two Testaments.

In the very last book of the Old Testament, Malachi, is recorded another significant prophecy: "Remember ye the law of Moses my servant, which I commanded unto him in Horeb for all Israel, even statutes and judgments. Behold, I will send you Elijah the prophet before the coming of the great and dreadful day of the LORD: and he shall turn the heart of the fathers to the children, and the heart of the children to their fathers, lest I come and smite the earth with a curse." Malachi 3:22-24. Here is a specific prediction made by a prophet of God. It is obvious this prophecy could not possibly have been fulfilled during the Old Testament dispensation, since Malachi is the last of the Old Testament prophets. Religious Jews, to this day, are awaiting the return of Elijah. Each Passover, during the Sedar service, an extra cup filled with wine, called "The Elijah Cup," is placed on the table; and following the meal, the door is opened in anticipation of Elijah's appearance.

In the New testament, we learn Malachi's prophecy has already been literally fulfilled, in part. "There was in the days of Herod, the King of Judea, a certain priest named Zacharias, of the course of Abia: and his wife was of the daughters of Aaron, and her name was Elisabeth. And they were both righteous before God, walking in all the commandments and ordinances of the Lord blameless. And they had no child, because that Elisabeth was barren and they both were now well stricken in years. And it came to pass, that while he executed the priest's office before God in the order of his course there were twenty-four courses in the Jewish priestly system in Bible times], according to the custom of the priest's office, his lot was to burn incense when he went into the temple of the Lord. And the whole multitude of the people were praying without at the time of incense. And there appeared unto him an angel of the Lord standing on the right side of the altar of incense. And when Zacharias saw him, he was troubled, and fear fell upon him. But the angel said unto him, Fear not, Zacharias: for thy prayer is heard; and thy wife Elisabeth shall bear thee a son, and thou shalt call his name John. For he shall be great in the sight of the Lord... And many of the children of Israel shall he turn to the Lord their God. And he shall go before him in the spirit and power of Elias, to turn the hearts of the fathers to the children, and the disobedient to the wisdom of the just; to make ready a people prepared for the Lord." Luke 1:5-13; 15-17.

One of the most outstanding Old Testament predictions is found in Deuteronomy 18:15-18, "The LORD thy God will raise up unto thee a prophet from the midst of thee, of thy brethren, like unto me; unto him ye shall hearken; according to all that thou desirest of the LORD thy God in Horeb in the day of the assembly, saying, Let me not hear again the voice of the LORD my God, neither let me see this great fire any more, that I die not. And the Lord said unto me, They have well spoken that which they have spoken. I will raise them up a prophet from among their brethren, like unto thee, and will put my words in his mouth; and he shall speak unto them all that I shall command him." It is very clear the revelation of divine truth by God to the people of Israel would be augmented by means of that great prophet whom He would raise up at some future time and that Israel should know the revelations given to His people by Moses alone would not suffice to fulfill His purposes for them. Futhermore, He warned His people to hearken unto that future prophet.

As we turn to the New Testament, we discover the full and complete fulfillment of the above prophecy of Moses. When our forefathers sent messengers to John the Baptist [**Johanan ham-Matbil,** or "John the Immerser"]-who administered to the repentant a rite of immersion; the Jewish ceremony of **Mikwah**-to inquire: "Who art thou? And he confessed and denied not, but he confessed thus: I am not The Messiah. And they asked: What then? Art thou Elijah? And he says: I am not. Art thou the Prophet? And he answered, No." John 1:19-21.

The Old Testament was first in proclaiming the Golden Rule, "Thou shalt love thy neighbor as thyself." Leviticus 19:18. The New Testament shows how comprehensive that rule is, pointing out our neighbor is not merely the person living next door to us, but any one who may be in need of the help we can give. Read Luke 10:30-37. We are informed it is God who gives us the power to increase our material possessions. Deuteronomy 8:18. The New Testament carries this thought still further by declaring the rich are God's stewards, whose duty it is to benefit those less favored-the poor, the underprivileged, the sick, the suffering. Under the influence of these teachings, many schools, hospitals, orphanages, homes for the aged, and centers of culture have been established in the darkest and most backward areas of the world.

Millions of dollars are donated and expended yearly by those who love God's Word, in order that the teachings of the divine principles, recorded in the Old and New Testaments, may be taught in the furthest corners of this earth. Thus it is that the knowledge of the God of Israel is gradually but surely covering earth's remotest bounds even as the waters cover the sea. Eternity alone will reveal the incalculable good accomplished by the circulation of the Holy Scriptures in all the languages of the world. Then, and only then, can we compute how many lives they have transformed, the hope they have engendered, the solace they have given, and the tears they have wiped away.

During the first 2500 years of human history no Bible existed— no collection of divine revelations were put down in written form. During that long period—more than one third of the history of the world—the Lord spoke to men through His prophets. These divine revelations of truth were cherished by the faithful and handed down orally from father to son. But as the time of the exodus of the children of Israel from Egypt drew near, and the darkness of paganism was becoming widely spread over the earth, the Lord saw fit to reveald truth in the writings we now call the Holy Scriptures. This work began with Moses. It was God's plan that with the passing of the centuries more and more truth should be revealed to His people through the prophets, and the body of revealed truth in written form should be augmented thereby. This was made known to Israel by the Lord.

What a cold, bleak, and desolate world this would be without the Bible! It is One Book that lightens the way. Its precious promises cheer us on to victory over our inherited and cultivated tendencies to evil. It points our path to a better world, even God's eternal kingdom where all will be light and joy, and where all that has baffled and perplexed us here will be made plain. Let us never cease to thank God for His beautiful love to us. His word, the Holy Scriptures- as we have learned, consist of the Old and the New Testaments. The God of Abraham has joined the two for our instruction that we might be edified, comforted, and blessed. The Bible in its entirety, consisting of both the Old and the New Testaments, is one of the most precious gifts heaven could bestow upon us. Both are in perfect agreement, and both of them form a perfect unity.

srh

Shalom

Peace

by

Ellen Gould White

Edited by
S. R. Howard

SAN® *Enterprises Inc.*
P. O. Box 623
Thorsby, AL 35171-0623

Cover Credits:
Cover by: Leah Berkowitz
Book Layout : Reesa Richman and Obidiah Markowitz

SAN® *Enterprises Inc.*
P. O. Box 623 • Thorsby, AL 35171

ISBN: 0-9621661-1-1

Printed in the U.S.A.

Contents

BOOK 2

SHALOM
PEACE

BOOK 2

SHALOM
PEACE

BY

ELLEN GOULD WHITE

*"Behold, I send an Angel before thee, to keep thee in
the way, and to bring thee into the place which I have
prepared."*

Exodus 23:20

CHAPTER 1

The Source Of Peace

NATURE AND REVELATION alike testify of God's
love. Our Father in heaven is the source of life, of wisdom,
and of joy. Look at the wonderful and beautiful things of
nature. Think of their marvelous adaptation to the needs and
happiness, not only of man, but of all living creatures. The
sunshine and the rain, that gladden and refresh the earth, the
hills and seas and plains, all speak to us of the Creator's love.
It is God who supplies the daily needs of all His creatures. In
the beautiful words of the psalmist,

> "The eyes of all wait upon Thee;
> And Thou givest them their meat in due season.
> Thou openest Thine hand,
> And satisfiest the desire of every living thing."
>
> Psalm 145:15, 16.

God made man perfectly holy and happy; and the fair earth,
as it came from the Creator's hand, bore no blight of decay or
shadow of the curse. It is transgression of God's law—the law
of love—that has brought woe and death. Yet even amid the
suffering that results from sin, God's love is revealed. It is
written that God cursed the ground for man's sake. Genesis
3:17. The thorn and the thistle—the difficulties and trials that
make his life one of toil and care—were appointed for his
good, as a part of the training needful in God's plan for his
uplifting from the ruin and degradation that sin has wrought.
The world, though fallen, is not all sorrow and misery. In
nature itself are messages of hope and comfort. There are
flowers upon the thistles, and the thorns are covered with roses.

"God is love," is written upon every opening bud, upon
every spire of springing grass. The lovely birds making the air
vocal with their happy songs, the delicately tinted flowers in
their perfection perfuming the air, the lofty trees of the forest
with their rich foliage of living green—all testify to the tender,
fatherly care of our God, and to His desire to make His children
happy

The Word of God reveals His character. He Himself has declared His infinite love and pity. When Moses prayed, "Show me Thy glory," the Lord answered, "I will make all My goodness pass before thee." Exodus 33:18, 19. This is His glory. The Lord passed before Moses, and proclaimed, "The Lord, The Lord God, merciful and gracious, long-suffering, and abundant in goodness and truth, keeping mercy for thousands, forgiving iniquity and transgression and sin." Exodus 34:6, 7. He is "slow to anger, and of great kindness," (Jonah 4:2), "because He delighteth in mercy." Micah 7:18.

God has bound our hearts to Him by unnumbered tokens in heaven and in earth. Through the things of nature, and the deepest and tenderest earthly ties that human hearts can know, He has sought to reveal Himself to us. Yet these but imperfectly represent His love. Though all these evidences have been given, the enemy of good blinded the minds of men, so that they looked upon God with fear; they thought of Him as severe and unforgiving. Satan led men to conceive of God as a being whose chief attribute is stern justice—one who is a severe judge, a harsh, exacting creditor. He pictured the Creator as a being who is watching with jealous eye to discern the errors and mistakes of men, that He may visit judgments upon them. It was to remove this dark shadow, by revealing to the world the infinite love of God, that The Redeemer came to live among men.

In describing His earthly mission, The Redeemer said, The Lord hath anointed Me to preach good news to the poor; He hath sent Me to heal the brokenhearted, to preach deliverance to the captives, and recovering of sight to the blind, to set at liberty them that are bruised.

This was His work. He went about doing good, and healing all that were oppressed by Satan. There were whole villages where there was not a moan of sickness in any house; for He had passed through them, and healed all their sick. His work gave evidence of His divine anointing. Love, mercy, and compassion were revealed in every act of His life; His heart went out in tender sympathy to the children of men. He took man's nature, that He might reach man's wants. The poorest and humblest were not afraid to approach Him. Even little children were attracted to Him. They loved to climb upon His knees, and gaze into the pensive face, benignant with love.

The Redeemer did not suppress one word of truth, but He uttered it always in love. He exercised the greatest tact, and thoughtful, kind attention, in His communion with the people. He was never rude, never needlessly spoke a severe word, never gave needless pain to a sensitive soul. He did not censure human weakness. He spoke the truth, but always in love. He denounced hypocrisy, unbelief, and iniquity; but tears were in His voice as He uttered His scathing rebukes. He wept over Jerusalem, the city He loved, which refused to receive Him, the Way, the Truth, and the Life. They had rejected Him, the Saviour, but He regarded them with pitying tenderness. His life was one of self-denial and thoughtful care for others. Every soul was precious in His eyes. While He ever bore Himself with divine dignity, He bowed with the tenderest regard to every member of the family of God. In all men He saw fallen souls whom it was His mission to save.

Such is the character of The Messiah as revealed in His life. This is the character of God. It is from the Father's heart that the streams of divine compassion, manifest in The Messiah , flow out to the children of men. The Redeemer, the tender, pitying Saviour, was God manifest in the flesh.

God permitted His beloved Son, full of grace and truth, to come from a world of indescribable glory, to a world marred and blighted with sin, darkened with the shadow of death and the curse. He permitted Him to leave the bosom of His love, the adoration of the angels, to suffer shame, insult, humiliation, hatred, and death. "The chastisement of our peace was upon Him; and with His stripes we are healed." Isaiah 53:5. The spotless Son of God took upon Himself the burden of sin. He who had been one with God, felt in His soul the awful separation that sin makes between God and man. This wrung from His lips the anguished cry, My God, My God, why hast Thou forsaken Me? It was the burden of sin, the sense of its terrible enormity, of its separation of the soul from God—it was this that broke His heart.

But this great sacrifice was not made in order to create in the Father's heart a love for man, not to make Him willing to save. No, no! God so loved the world, that He gave His only begotten Son. The Father loves us, not because of the great provision but He provided the provision because He loves us. The Messiah was the medium through which He could pour out His infinite love upon a fallen world. God was in The Messiah, reconciling the world unto Himself. God suffered with His Son.

None but The Messiah could accomplish our redemption; for only He who was in the bosom of the Father could declare

Him. Only He who knew the height and depth of the love of God could make it manifest. Nothing less than the infinite sacrifice made by The Messiah in behalf of fallen man could express the Father's love to lost humanity.

God so loved the world, that He gave His only begotten Son. He gave Him not only to live among men, to bear their sins, and die their sacrifice. He gave Him to the fallen race. The Messiah was to identify Himself with the interests and needs of humanity. He who was one with God has linked Himself with the children of men by ties that are never to be broken. The Redeemer is not ashamed to call us brethren; He is our Sacrifice, our Advocate, our Brother, bearing our human form before the Father's throne, and through eternal ages one with the race He has redeemed—the Son of man. And all this that man might be uplifted from the ruin and degradation of sin that he might reflect the love of God, and share the joy of holiness.

The price paid for our redemption, the infinite sacrifice of our heavenly Father in giving His Son to die for us, should give us exalted conceptions of what we may become through The Messiah. John beheld the height, the depth, the breadth of the Father's love toward the perishing race, he was filled with adoration and reverence; and, failing to find suitable language in which to express the greatness and tenderness of this love, he called upon the world to behold it. Behold, what manner of love the Father hath bestowed upon us, that we should be called the sons of God. What a value this places upon man! Through transgression, the sons of man become subjects of Satan. Through faith in the atoning sacrifice of The Messiah, the sons of Adam may become the sons of God. By assuming human nature, The Messiah elevates humanity. Fallen men are placed where, through connection with The Messiah, they may indeed become worthy of the name "sons of God."

Such love is without a parallel. Children of the heavenly King! Precious promise! Theme for the most profound meditation! The matchless love of God for a world that did not love Him! The thought has a subduing power upon the soul, and brings the mind into captivity to the will of God. The more we study the divine character in the light of the cross, the more we see mercy, tenderness, and forgiveness blended with equity and justice, and the more clearly we discern innumerable evidences of a love that is infinite, and a tender pity surpassing a mother's yearning sympathy for her wayward child.

CHAPTER 2

Your Need For Peace

MAN WAS ORIGINALLY endowed with noble powers and a well-balanced mind. He was perfect in his being, and in harmony with God. His thoughts were pure, his aims holy. But through disobedience, his powers were perverted, and selfishness took the place of love. His nature became so weakened through transgression that it was impossible for him, in his own strength, to resist the power of evil. He was made captive by Satan, and would have remained so forever had not God specially interposed. It was the tempter's purpose to thwart the divine plan in man's creation, and fill the earth with woe and desolation. And he would point to all this evil as the result of God's work in creating man.

In his sinless state, man held joyful communion with Him in whom are hid all the treasures of wisdom and knowledge. But after his sin, he could no longer find joy in holiness, and he sought to hide from the presence of God. Such is still the condition of the unrenewed heart. It is not in harmony with God, and finds no joy in communion with Him. The sinner could not be happy in God's presence; he would shrink from the companionship of holy beings. Could he be permitted to enter heaven, it would have no joy for him. The spirit of unselfish love that reigns there—every heart responding to the heart of Infinite Love—would touch no answering chord in his soul. His thoughts, his interests, his motives, would be alien to those that actuate the sinless dwellers there. He would be a discordant note in the melody of heaven. Heaven would be to him a place of torture; he would long to be hidden from Him who is its light, and the center of its joy. It is no arbitrary decree on the part of God that excludes the wicked from heaven: they are shut out by their own unfitness for its companionship. The glory of God would be to them a consuming fire. They would welcome destruction, that they might be hidden from the face of Him who died to redeem them.

It is impossible for us, of ourselves, to escape from the pit of sin in which we are sunken. Our hearts are evil, and we cannot change them. "Who can bring a clean thing out of an unclean? not one." Job 14:4. Education, culture, the exercise of the will, human effort, all have their proper sphere, but here they are powerless. They may produce an outward correctness of behavior, but they cannot change the heart; they cannot purify the springs of life. There must be a power working from within, a new life from above, before men can be changed from sin to holiness. That power is The Messiah. His grace alone can quicken the lifeless faculties of the soul, and attract it to God, to holiness.

It is not enough to perceive the loving-kindness of God, to see the benevolence, the fatherly tenderness, of His character. It is not enough to discern the wisdom and justice of His law, to see that it is founded upon the eternal principle of love. Paul saw all this when he exclaimed, I consent unto the law that it is good. The law is holy, and the commandment holy, and just, and good. But he added, in the bitterness of his soul-anguish and despair, I am carnal, sold under sin. He longed for the purity, the righteousness, to which in himself he was powerless to attain, and he cried out, O wretched man that I am! who shall deliver me from this body of death? Such is the cry that has gone up from burdened hearts in all lands and in all ages. To all, there is but one answer, Behold the Lamb of God, which taketh away the sin of the world.

Many are the figures by which the Spirit of God has sought to illustrate this truth, and make it plain to souls that long to be freed from the burden of guilt. When, after his sin in deceiving Esau, Jacob fled from his father's home, he was weighed down with a sense of guilt. Lonely and outcast as he was, separated from all that had made life dear, the one thought that above all others pressed upon his soul, was the fear that his sin had cut him off from God, that he was forsaken of Heaven. In sadness he lay down to rest on the bare earth, around him only the lonely hills, and above, the heavens bright with stars. As he slept, a strange light broke upon his vision; and lo, from the plain on which he lay, vast shadowy stairs seemed to lead upward to the very gates of heaven, and upon them angels of God were passing up and down; while from the glory above, the divine voice was heard in a message of comfort and hope. Thus was made known to Jacob that which met the need and longing of his soul—a Saviour. With joy and gratitude he saw revealed a way by which he, a sinner, could be restored to communion with God. The mystic ladder of his dream represented The Redeemer, the only medium of communication between God and man.

In the apostasy, man alienated himself from God; earth was cut off from heaven. Across the gulf that lay between, there could be no communion. But through The Messiah, earth is again linked with heaven. With His own merits, The Messiah has bridged the gulf which sin had made, so that the ministering angels can hold communion with man. The Messiah connects fallen man in his weakness and helplessness with the Source of infinite power.

But in vain are men's dreams of progress, in vain all efforts for the uplifting of humanity, if they neglect the one Source of hope and help for the fallen race. Every good gift and every perfect gift, is from God. There is no true excellence of character apart from Him. And the only way to God is The Messiah.

The heart of God yearns over His earthly children with a love stronger than death. In giving up His Son, He has poured out to us all heaven in one gift. The Saviour's life and death and intercession, the ministry of angels, the pleading of the Spirit, the Father working above and through all, the unceasing interest of heavenly beings—all are enlisted in behalf of man's redemption.

O let us contemplate the amazing sacrifice that has been made for us! Let us try to appreciate the labor and energy that Heaven is expending to reclaim the lost, and bring them back to the Father's house. Motives stronger, and agencies more powerful, could never be brought into operation; the exceeding rewards for right-doing, the enjoyment of heaven, the society of the angels, the communion and love of God and His Son, the elevation and extension of all our powers throughout eternal ages—are these not mighty incentives and encouragements to urge us to give the heart's loving service to our Creator and Redeemer?

And, on the other hand, the judgments of God pronounced against sin, the inevitable retribution, the degradation of our character, and the final destruction are presented in God's Word to warn us against the service of Satan.

Shall we not regard the mercy of God? What more could He do? Let us place ourselves in right relation to Him who has loved us with amazing love. Let us avail ourselves of the means provided for us that we may be transformed into His likeness, and be restored to fellowship with the ministering angels, to harmony and communion with the Father and the Son.

CHAPTER 3

The Guilt Factor

HOW SHALL A MAN be just with God? How shall the sinner be made righteous? It is only through The Messiah that we can be brought into harmony with God, with holiness; but how are we to come to The Messiah? Many are asking the same question as did the multitude on the Day of Pentecost, when, convicted of sin, they cried out, What shall we do? Repent, says The Messiah.

Repentance includes sorrow for sin, and a turning away from it. We shall not renounce sin unless we see its sinfulness; until we turn away from it in heart, there will be no real change in the life.

There are many who fail to understand the true nature of repentance. Multitudes sorrow that they have sinned, and even make an outward reformation, because they fear that their wrongdoing will bring suffering upon themselves. But this is not repentance in the Bible sense. They lament the suffering, rather than the sin. Such was the grief of Esau when he saw that the birthright was lost to him forever. Balaam, terrified by the angel standing in his pathway with drawn sword, acknowledged his guilt lest he should lose his life; but there was no genuine repentance for sin, no conversion of purpose, no abhorrence of evil. Judas , after betraying The Messiah , exclaimed, I have sinned in that I have betrayed the innocent blood. Pharaoh, when suffering under the judgments of God, acknowledged his sin in order to escape further punishment, but returned to his defiance of Heaven as soon as the plagues were stayed. These all lamented the results of sin, but did not sorrow for the sin itself.

But when the heart yields to the influence of the Spirit of God, the conscience will be quickened, and the sinner will discern something of the depth and sacredness of God's holy law, the foundation of His government in heaven and on earth. The Light which lighteth every man that cometh into the world, illumines the secret chambers of the soul, and the hidden things of darkness are made manifest. Conviction takes hold upon the mind and heart. The sinner has a sense of the righteousness of

14

Jehovah, and feels the terror of appearing, in his own guilt and uncleanness, before the Searcher of hearts. He sees the love of God, the beauty of holiness, the joy of purity; he longs to be cleansed, and to be restored to communion with Heaven.

The prayer of David after his fall, illustrates the nature of true sorrow for sin. His repentance was sincere and deep. There was no effort to palliate his guilt; no desire to escape the judgment threatened, inspired his prayer. David saw the enormity of his transgression; he saw the defilement of his soul; he loathed his sin. It was not for pardon only that he prayed, but for purity of heart. He longed for the joy of holiness—to be restored to harmony and communion with God. This was the language of his soul:

"Blessed is he whose transgression is forgiven, whose sin is
covered.
Blessed is the man unto whom the Lord imputeth not
iniquity,
And in whose spirit there is no guile."
                                        Psalm 32:1, 2.

"Have mercy upon me, O God, according to Thy
lovingkindness:
According unto the multitude of Thy tender mercies blot
out my transgressions....
For I acknowledge my transgressions: and my sin is ever
before me....
Purge me with hyssop, and I shall be clean: wash me, and I
shall be whiter than snow....

Create in me a clean heart, O God;
And renew a right spirit within me.
Cast me not away from Thy presence;
And take not Thy Holy Spirit from me.
Restore unto me the joy of Thy salvation;
And uphold me with Thy free spirit....
Deliver me from bloodguiltiness, O God, Thou God of my
salvation!
And my tongue shall sing aloud of Thy righteousness."
                                        Psalm 51:1-14.

A repentance such as this, is beyond the reach of our own
power to accomplish; it is obtained only from The Messiah,
who ascended up on high, and has given gifts unto men.

Just here is a point on which many may err, and hence they
fail of receiving the help that The Messiah desires to give them.
They think that they cannot come to The Messiah unless they
first repent, and that repentance prepares for the forgiveness of
their sins.   It is true that repentance does precede the
forgiveness of sins; for it is only the broken and contrite heart
that will feel the need of a Saviour. But must the sinner wait
till he has repented before he can come to The Redeemer? Is
repentance to be made an obstacle between the sinner and The
Saviour?

The Bible does not teach that the sinner must repent before
he can heed the invitation of The Messiah, Come unto Me, all
ye that labor and are heavy laden, and I will give you rest. It is
the virtue that goes forth from The Messiah, that leads to
genuine repentance. We can no more repent without the Spirit
of The Messiah to awaken the conscience than we can be
pardoned without The Messiah.

The Messiah is the source of every right impulse. He is the
only one that can implant in the heart enmity against sin.
Every desire for truth and purity, every conviction of our own
sinfulness, is an evidence that His Spirit is moving upon our
hearts.

The Messiah must be revealed to the sinner as the Saviour
dying for the sins of the world; and as we behold the Lamb of
God upon the cross of Calvary, the mystery of redemption
begins to unfold to our minds, and the goodness of God leads
us to repentance. In dying for sinners, The Messiah manifested
a love that is incomprehensible; and as the sinner beholds this
love, it softens the heart, impresses the mind, and inspires
contrition in the soul.

It is true that men sometimes become ashamed of their
sinful ways, and give up some of their evil habits, before they
are conscious that they are being drawn to The Messiah. But
whenever they make an effort to reform, from a sincere desire
to do right, it is the power of The Messiah that is drawing them.
An influence of which they are unconscious works upon the
soul, and the conscience is quickened, and the outward life is
amended. And as The Messiah draws them to look upon Him,
to behold Him whom their sins have pierced, the

commandment comes home to the conscience. The wickedness of their life, the deep-seated sin of the soul, is revealed to them. They begin to comprehend something of the righteousness of The Messiah, and exclaim, "What is sin, that it should require such a sacrifice for the redemption of its victim? Was all this love, all this suffering, all this humiliation demanded, that we might not perish, but have everlasting life?"

The sinner may resist this love, may refuse to be drawn to The Messiah; but if he does not resist, he will be drawn to The Redeemer; a knowledge of the plan of salvation will lead him to seek The Messiah for repentance for his sins, which have caused the sufferings of God's dear Son.

The same divine mind that is working upon the things of nature is speaking to the hearts of men, and creating an inexpressible craving for something they have not. The things of the world cannot satisfy their longing. The Spirit of God is pleading with them to seek for those things that alone can give peace and rest—the grace of The Messiah, the joy of holiness. Through influences seen and unseen, our Saviour is constantly at work to attract the minds of men from the unsatisfying pleasures of sin to the infinite blessings that may be theirs in Him. To all these souls, who are vainly seeking to drink from the broken cisterns of this world, the divine message is addressed, Let him that is athirst come. And whosoever will, let him take the water of life freely.

You who in heart long for something better than this world can give, recognize this longing as the voice of God to your soul. Ask Him to give you repentance, to reveal The Messiah to you in His infinite love, in His perfect purity. In The Saviour's life the principles of God's law—love to God and man—were perfectly exemplified. Benevolence, unselfish love, was the life of His soul. It is as we behold Him, as the light from our Saviour falls upon us, that we see the sinfulness of our own hearts.

We may have flattered ourselves, as did Nicodemus, that our life has been upright, that our moral character is correct, and think that we need not humble the heart before God, like the common sinner: but when the light from The Messiah shines into our souls, we shall see how impure we are; we shall discern the selfishness of motive, the enmity against God, that has defiled every act of life. Then we shall know that our own righteousness is indeed as filthy rags, and that the blood of The

Messiah alone can cleanse us from the defilement of sin, and
renew our hearts in His own likeness.

One ray of the glory of God, one gleam of the purity of The
Messiah, penetrating the soul, makes every spot of defilement
painfully distinct, and lays bare the deformity and defects of
the human character.   It makes apparent the unhallowed
desires, the infidelity of the heart, the impurity of the lips. The
sinner's acts of disloyalty in making void the law of God, are
exposed to his sight, and his spirit is stricken and afflicted
under the searching influence of the Spirit of God. He loathes
himself as he views the pure, spotless character of The
Messiah.

When the prophet Daniel beheld the glory surrounding the
heavenly messenger that was sent unto him, he was
overwhelmed with a sense of his own weakness and
imperfection. Describing the effect of the wonderful scene, he
says, "There remained no strength in me: for my comeliness
was turned in me into corruption, and I retained no strength."
Daniel 10:8. The soul thus touched will hate its selfishness,
abhor its self-love, and will seek, through The Messiah's
righteousness, for the purity of heart that is in harmony with
the law of God and the character of The Messiah.

Paul says that as touching the righteousness which is in the
law—as far as outward acts were concerned—he was
blameless; but when the spiritual character of the law was
discerned, he saw himself a sinner. Judged by the letter of the
law as men apply it to the outward life, he had abstained from
sin; but when he looked into the depths of its holy precepts, and
saw himself as God saw him, he bowed in humiliation, and
confessed his guilt. I was alive without the law once: but when
the commandment came, sin revived, and I died. When he saw
the spiritual nature of the law, sin appeared in its true
hideousness, and his self-esteem was gone.

God does not regard all sin as of equal magnitude; there are
degrees of guilt in His estimation, as well as in that of man; but
however trifling this or that wrong act may seem in the eyes of
men, no sin is small in the sight of God. Man's judgment is
partial, imperfect; but God estimates all things as they really
are. The drunkard is despised, and is told that his sin will
exclude him from heaven; while pride, selfishness, and
covetousness too often go unrebuked. But these are sins that
are especially offensive to God; for they are contrary to the

benevolence of His character, to that unselfish love which is the very atmosphere of the unfallen universe. He who falls into some of the grosser sins may feel a sense of his shame and poverty and his need of the grace of The Messiah; but pride feels no need, and so it closes the heart against The Messiah, and the infinite blessings He came to give.

If you see your sinfulness, do not wait to make yourself better. How many there are who think they are not good enough to come to The Messiah. Do you expect to become better through your own efforts? "Can the Ethiopian change his skin, or the leopard his spots? then may ye also do good, that are accustomed to do evil." Jeremiah 13:23. There is help for us only in God. We must not wait for stronger persuasions, for better opportunities, or for holier tempers. We can do nothing of ourselves. We must come to The Messiah just as we are.

But let none deceive themselves with the thought that God, in His great love and mercy, will yet save even the rejectors of His grace. The exceeding sinfulness of sin can be estimated only in the light of the cross. When men urge that God is too good to cast off the sinner, let them look to Calvary. It was because there was no other way in which man could be saved, because without this sacrifice it was impossible for the human race to escape from the defiling power of sin, and be restored to communion with holy beings—impossible for them again to become partakers of spiritual life—it was because of this that The Messiah took upon Himself the guilt of the disobedient, and suffered in the sinner's stead. The love and suffering and death of the Son of God all testify to the terrible enormity of sin, and declare that there is no escape from its power, no hope of the higher life, but through the submission of the soul to The Messiah.

The impenitent sometimes excuse themselves by saying of professed Believers, "I am as good as they are. They are no more self-denying, sober, or circumspect in their conduct than I am. They love pleasure and self-indulgence as well as I do." Thus they make the faults of others an excuse for their own neglect of duty. But the sins and defects of others do not excuse anyone; for the Lord has not given us an erring human pattern. The spotless Messiah has been given as our example, and those who complain of the wrong course of professed Believers are the ones who should show better lives and nobler examples. If they have so high a conception of what a Believer should be, is not their own sin so much the greater? They know what is right, and yet refuse to do it.

Beware of procrastination. Do not put off the work of forsaking your sins, and seeking purity of heart through The Redeemer. Here is where thousands upon thousands have erred, to their eternal loss. I will not here dwell upon the shortness and uncertainty of life; but there is a terrible danger—a danger not sufficiently understood—in delaying to yield to the pleading voice of God's Holy Spirit, in choosing to live in sin; for such this delay really is. Sin, however small it may be esteemed, can be indulged in only at the peril of infinite loss. What we do not overcome, will overcome us, and work out our destruction.

Adam and Eve persuaded themselves that in so small a matter as eating of the forbidden fruit, there could not result such terrible consequences as God had declared. But this small matter was the transgression of God's immutable and holy law, and it separated man from God, and opened the floodgates of death and untold woe upon our world. Age after age there has gone up from our earth a continual cry of mourning, and the whole creation groaneth and travaileth together in pain, as a consequence of man's disobedience. Heaven itself has felt the effects of his rebellion against God. Let us not regard sin as a trivial thing.

Every act of transgression, every neglect or rejection of the grace of The Messiah, is reacting upon yourself; it is hardening the heart, depraving the will, benumbing the understanding, and not only making you less inclined to yield, but less capable of yielding, to the tender pleading of God's Holy Spirit.

Many are quieting a troubled conscience with the thought that they can change a course of evil when they choose; that they can trifle with the invitations of mercy, and yet be again and again impressed. They think that after doing despite to the Spirit of grace, after casting their influence on the side of Satan, in a moment of terrible extremity they can change their course. But this is not so easily done. The experience, the education, of a lifetime, has so thoroughly molded the character that few then desire to receive the image of The Redeemer.

Even one wrong trait of character, one sinful desire, persistently cherished, will eventually neutralize all the power of the good news. Every sinful indulgence strengthens the soul's aversion to God. The man who manifests an infidel hardihood, or a stolid indifference to divine truth, is but reaping the harvest of that which he has himself sown. In all the Bible there is not a more fearful warning against trifling with evil than the words of the wise man, that the sinner "shall be holden with the cords of his sins." Proverbs 5:22.

The Messiah is ready to set us free from sin, but He does not force the will; and if by persistent transgression the will itself is wholly bent on evil, and we do not desire to be set free, if we will not accept His grace, what more can He do? We have destroyed ourselves by our determined rejection of His love.

"Man looketh on the outward appearance, but the Lord looketh on the heart"—the human heart, with its conflicting emotions of joy and sorrow; the wandering, wayward heart, which is the abode of so much impurity and deceit. 1 Samuel 16:7. He knows its motives, its very intents and purposes. Go to Him with your soul all stained as it is. Like the psalmist, throw its chambers open to the all-seeing eye, exclaiming, "Search me, O God, and know my heart: try me, and know my thoughts: and see if there be any wicked way in me, and lead me in the way everlasting." Psalm 139:23, 24.

Many accept an intellectual religion, a form of godliness, when the heart is not cleansed. Let it be your prayer, "Create in me a clean heart, O God; and renew a right spirit within me." Psalm 51:10. Deal truly with your own soul. Be as earnest, as persistent, as you would be if your mortal life were at stake. This is a matter to be settled between God and your own soul, settled for eternity. A supposed hope, and nothing more, will prove your ruin.

Study God's word prayerfully. That word presents before you, in the law of God and the life of The Messiah, the great principles of holiness, without which no man shall see the Lord. It convinces of sin; it plainly reveals the way of salvation. Give heed to it, as the voice of God speaking to your soul.

As you see the enormity of sin, as you see yourself as you really are, do not give up to despair. It was sinners that The Messiah came to save. We have not to reconcile God to us, but—O wondrous love!—God in The Messiah is reconciling the world unto Himself. He is wooing by His tender love the hearts of His erring children. No earthly parent could be as patient with the faults and mistakes of his children, as is God with those He seeks to save. No one could plead more tenderly with the transgressor. No human lips ever poured out more tender entreaties to the wanderer than does He. All His promises, His warnings, are but the breathing of unutterable love.

When Satan comes to tell you that you are a great sinner, look up to your Redeemer, and talk of His merits. That which will help you is to look to His light. Acknowledge your sin, but tell the enemy that The Messiah-Redeemer came into the world to save sinners, and that you may be saved by His matchless love. We have been great sinners, but The Messiah died that we might be forgiven. The merits of His sacrifice are sufficient to present to the Father in our behalf. Those to whom He has forgiven most will love Him most, and will stand nearest to His throne to praise Him for His great love and infinite sacrifice. It is when we most fully comprehend the love of God that we best realize the sinfulness of sin. When we see the length of the chain that was let down for us, when we understand something of the infinite sacrifice that The Messiah has made in our behalf, the heart is melted with tenderness and contrition.

CHAPTER 4

Living With Your Conscience

"HE THAT COVERETH his sins shall not prosper: but whoso confesseth and forsaketh them shall have mercy." Proverbs 28:13.

The conditions of obtaining mercy of God are simple and just and reasonable. The Lord does not require us to do some grievous thing in order that we may have the forgiveness of sin. We need not make long and wearisome pilgrimages, or perform painful penances, to commend our souls to the God of heaven or to expiate our transgression; but he that confesseth and forsaketh his sin shall have mercy.

Confess your sins to God, who only can forgive them, and your faults to one another. If you have given offense to your friend or neighbor, you are to acknowledge your wrong, and it is his duty freely to forgive you. Then you are to seek the forgiveness of God, because the brother you have wounded is the property of God, and in injuring him you sinned against his Creator and Redeemer. The case is brought before the only true Mediator, our great High Priest, who was in all points tempted like as we are, yet without sin, and who is touched with the feeling of our infirmities, and is able to cleanse from every stain of iniquity.

Those who have not humbled their souls before God in acknowledging their guilt, have not yet fulfilled the first condition of acceptance. If we have not experienced that repentance which is not to be repented of, and have not with true humiliation of soul and brokenness of spirit confessed our sins, abhorring our iniquity, we have never truly sought for the forgiveness of sin; and if we have never sought, we have never found the peace of God. The only reason why we do not have remission of sins that are past is that we are not willing to humble our hearts and comply with the conditions of the word of truth. Explicit instruction is given concerning this matter. Confession of sin, whether public or private, should be heartfelt, and freely expressed. It is not to be urged from the sinner. It is not to be made in a flippant and careless way, or forced from those who have no realizing sense of the abhorrent character of sin. The confession that is the outpouring of the inmost soul finds its way to the God of infinite pity. The psalmist says, "The Lord is nigh unto them that are of a broken heart; and saveth such as be of a contrite spirit." Psalm 34:18.

True confession is always of a specific character, and acknowledges particular sins. They may be of such a nature as to be brought before God only; they may be wrongs that should be confessed to individuals who have suffered injury through them; or they may be of a public character, and should then be as publicly confessed. But all confession should be definite and to the point, acknowledging the very sins of which you are guilty.

In the days of Samuel, the Israelites wandered from God. They were suffering the consequences of sin; for they had lost their faith in God, lost their discernment of His power and wisdom to rule the nation, lost their confidence in His ability to defend and vindicate His cause. They turned from the great Ruler of the universe, and desired to be governed as were the nations around them. Before they found peace, they made this definite confession: "We have added unto all our sins this evil, to ask us a king." 1 Samuel 12:19. The very sin of which they were convicted had to be confessed. Their ingratitude oppressed their souls, and severed them from God.

Confession will not be acceptable to God without sincere repentance and reformation. There must be decided changes in the life; everything offensive to God must be put away. This will be the result of genuine sorrow for sin. The work that we have to do on our part is plainly set before us: "Wash you, make you clean; put away the evil of your doings from before Mine eyes; cease to do evil; learn to do well; seek judgment, relieve the oppressed, judge the fatherless, plead for the widow." Isaiah 1:16, 17. "If the wicked restore the pledge, give again that he had robbed, walk in the statutes of life, without committing iniquity; he shall surely live, he shall not die." Ezekiel 33:15.

When sin has deadened the moral perceptions, the wrongdoer does not discern the defects of his character, nor realize the enormity of the evil he has committed; and unless he yields to the convicting power of the Holy Spirit, he remains in partial blindness to his sin. His confessions are not sincere and in earnest. To every acknowledgment of his guilt he adds an apology in excuse of his course, declaring that if it had not been for certain circumstances, he would not have done this or that, for which he is reproved.

After Adam and Eve had eaten of the forbidden fruit, they were filled with a sense of shame and terror. At first their only thought was how to excuse their sin, and escape the dreaded sentence of death. When the Lord inquired concerning their sin, Adam replied, laying the guilt partly upon God and partly upon his companion: "The woman whom Thou gavest to be with me, she gave me of the tree, and I did eat." The woman put the blame upon the serpent, saying, "The serpent beguiled me, and I did eat." Genesis 3:12, 13. Why did You make the serpent? Why did You suffer him to come into Eden? These were the questions implied in her excuse for her sin, thus charging God with the responsibility of their fall. The spirit of self-justification originated in the father of lies, and has been exhibited by all the sons and daughters of Adam. Confessions of this order are not inspired by the divine Spirit, and will not be acceptable to God. True repentance will lead a man to bear his guilt himself, and acknowledge it without deception or hypocrisy. Like the poor man not lifting up so much as his eyes unto heaven, he will cry, God be merciful to me a sinner; and those who do acknowledge their guilt will be justified; for The Redeemer will plead His blood in behalf of the repentant soul. The examples in God's Word of genuine repentance and humiliation reveal a spirit of confession in which there is no excuse for sin or attempt at self-justification.

CHAPTER 5

Life At Its Best

GOD'S PROMISE IS, "Ye shall seek Me, and find Me, when ye shall search for Me with all your heart." Jeremiah 29:13.

The whole heart must be yielded to God, or the change can never be wrought in us by which we are to be restored to His likeness. By nature we are alienated from God. The Holy Spirit describes our condition in such words as these: "the whole head is sick, and the whole heart faint;" "no soundness in it." Isaiah 1:5, 6. We are held fast in the snare of Satan; taken captive by him at his will. God desires to heal us, to set us free. But since this requires an entire transformation, a renewing of our whole nature, we must yield ourselves wholly to Him.

The warfare against self is the greatest battle that was ever fought. The yielding of self, surrendering all to the will of God, requires a struggle; but the soul must submit to God before it can be renewed in holiness.

The government of God is not, as Satan would make it appear, founded upon a blind submission, an unreasoning control. It appeals to the intellect and the conscience. "Come now, and let us reason together," (Isaiah 1:18), is the Creator's invitation to the beings He has made. God does not force the will of His creatures. He cannot accept an homage that is not willingly and intelligently given. A mere forced submission would prevent all real development of mind or character; it would make man a mere automaton. Such is not the purpose of the Creator. He desires that man, the crowning work of His creative power, shall reach the highest possible development. He sets before us the height of blessing to which He desires to bring us through His grace. He invites us to give ourselves to Him, that He may work His will in us. It remains for us to choose whether we will be set free from the bondage of sin, to share the glorious liberty of the sons of God.

In giving ourselves to God, we must necessarily give up all that would separate us from Him. Whatever shall draw away the heart from God must be given up. Mammon is the idol of

26

many. The love of money, the desire for wealth, is the golden chain that binds them to Satan. Reputation and worldly honor are worshiped by another class. The life of selfish ease and freedom from responsibility is the idol of others. But these slavish bands must be broken. We cannot be half the Lord's and half the world's. We are not God's children unless we are such entirely.

There are those who profess to serve God, while they rely upon their own efforts to obey His law, to form a right character, and secure salvation. Their hearts are not moved by any deep sense of the love of The Messiah, but they seek to perform the duties of the Believers' life as that which God requires of them in order to gain heaven. Such religion is worth nothing. When The Messiah dwells in the heart, the soul will be so filled with His love, with the joy of communion with Him, that it will cleave to Him; and in the contemplation of Him, self will be forgotten. Love to The Messiah will be the spring of action. Those who feel the constraining love of God, do not ask how little may be given to meet the requirements of God; they do not ask for the lowest standard, but aim at perfect conformity to the will of their Redeemer. With earnest desire they yield all, and manifest an interest proportionate to the value of the object which they seek. A profession of The Messiah without this deep love, is mere talk, dry formality, and heavy drudgery.

Do you feel that it is too great a sacrifice to yield all to The Messiah? Ask yourself the question. What has The Messiah given for me? The Son of God gave all—life and love and suffering—for our redemption. And can it be that we, the unworthy objects of so great love, will withhold our hearts from Him? Every moment of our lives we have been partakers of the blessings of His grace, and for this very reason we cannot fully realize the depths of ignorance and misery from which we have been saved. Can we look upon Him whom our sins have pierced, and yet be willing to do despite to all His love and sacrifice? In view of the infinite humiliation of the Lord of glory, shall we murmur because we can enter into life only through conflict and self-abasement?

The inquiry of many a proud heart is, "Why need I go in penitence and humiliation before I can have the assurance of my acceptance with God?" I point you to The Messiah. He was sinless, and, more than this, He was the Prince of heaven; but in man's behalf He became sin for the race. "He was numbered with the transgressors; and He bare the sin of many, and made intercession for the transgressors." Isaiah 53:12.

But what do we give up, when we give all? A sin-polluted heart, for The Redeemer to purify, to cleanse by His own blood, and to save by His matchless love. And yet men think it hard to give up all! I am ashamed to hear it spoken of, ashamed to write it.

God does not require us to give up anything that it is for our best interest to retain. In all that He does, He has the well-being of His children in view. Would that all who have not chosen The Messiah might realize that He has something vastly better to offer them than they are seeking for themselves. Man is doing the greatest injury and injustice to his own soul when he thinks and acts contrary to the will of God. No real joy can be found in the path forbidden by Him who knows what is best, and who plans for the good of His creatures. The path of transgression is the path of misery and destruction.

It is a mistake to entertain the thought that God is pleased to see His children suffer. All heaven is interested in the happiness of man. Our heavenly Father does not close the avenues of joy to any of His creatures. The divine requirements call upon us to shun those indulgences that would bring suffering and disappointment, that would close to us the door of happiness and heaven. The world's Redeemer accepts men as they are, with all their wants, imperfections, and weaknesses; and He will not only cleanse from sin and grant redemption through His blood, but will satisfy the heart-longing of all who consent to wear His yoke, to bear His burden. It is His purpose to impart peace and rest to all who come to Him for the bread of life. He requires us to perform only those duties that will lead our steps to heights of bliss to which the disobedient can never attain. The true, joyous life of the soul is to have The Messiah formed within, the hope of glory.

Many are inquiring, "How am I to make the surrender of myself to God?" You desire to give yourself to Him, but you are weak in moral power, in slavery to doubt, and controlled by the habits of your life of sin. Your promises and resolutions are like ropes of sand. You cannot control your thoughts, your impulses, your affections. The knowledge of your broken promises and forfeited pledges weakens your confidence in your own sincerity, and causes you to feel that God cannot accept you; but you need not despair. What you need to understand is the true force of the will. This is the governing power in the nature of man, the power of decision, or of choice. Everything depends on the right action of the will. The power of choice God has given to men; it is theirs to exercise. You cannot change your heart, you cannot of yourself give to God its affections; but you can choose to serve Him. You can give Him your will; He will then work in you to will and to do according to His good pleasure. Thus your whole nature will be brought under the control of the Spirit of The Messiah; your affections will be centered upon Him, your thoughts will be in harmony with Him.

Desires for goodness and holiness are right as far as they go; but if you stop here, they will avail nothing. Many will be lost while hoping and desiring to be Believers. They do not come to the point of yielding the will to God. They do not now choose to be Believers.

Through the right exercise of the will, an entire change may be made in your life. By yielding up your will to The Messiah, you ally yourself with the power that is above all principalities and powers. You will have strength from above to hold you steadfast, and thus through constant surrender to God you will be enabled to live the new life, even the life of faith.

CHAPTER 6

The Role of Faith

AS YOUR CONSCIENCE has been quickened by the Holy Spirit, you have seen something of the evil of sin, of its power, its guilt, its woe; and you look upon it with abhorrence. You feel that sin has separated you from God, that you are in bondage to the power of evil. The more you struggle to escape, the more you realize your helplessness. Your motives are impure; your heart is unclean. You see that your life has been filled with selfishness and sin. You long to be forgiven, to be cleansed, to be set free. Harmony with God, likeness to Him—what can you do to obtain it?

It is peace that you need—Heaven's forgiveness and peace and love in the soul. Money cannot buy it, intellect cannot procure it, wisdom cannot attain to it; you can never hope, by your own efforts, to secure it. But God offers it to you as a gift, "without money and without price." Isaiah 55:1. It is yours if you will but reach out your hand and grasp it. The Lord says, "Though your sins be as scarlet, they shall be as white as snow; though they be red like crimson, they shall be as wool." Isaiah 1:18. "A new heart also will I give you, and a new spirit will I put within you." Ezekiel 36:26.

You have confessed your sins, and in heart put them away. You have resolved to give yourself to God. Now go to Him, and ask that He will wash away your sins, and give you a new heart. Then believe that He does this because He has promised. This is the lesson which The Redeemer taught while He was on earth, that the gift which God promises us, we must believe we do receive, and it is ours. The Redeemer healed the people of their diseases when they had faith in His power; He helped them in the things which they could see, thus inspiring them with confidence in Him concerning things which they could not see—leading them to believe in His power to forgive sins. This He plainly stated in the healing of the man sick with palsy: That ye may know that the Son of man hath power on earth to forgive sins (then saith He to the sick of the palsy), Arise, take up thy bed, and go unto thine house.

From the simple Bible account of how The Redeemer healed the sick, we may learn something about how to believe in Him for the forgiveness of sins. Let us turn to the story of the paralytic at Bethesda. The poor sufferer was helpless; he had not used his limbs for thirty-eight years. Yet The Redeemer bade him, Rise, take up thy bed, and walk. The sick man might have said, Lord, if Thou wilt make me whole, I will obey Thy word. But no, he believed The Messiah's word, believed that he was made whole, and he made the effort at once; he willed to walk, and he did walk. He acted on the word of The Messiah, and God gave the power. He was made whole.

In like manner you are a sinner. You cannot atone for your past sins, you cannot change your heart, and make yourself holy. But God promises to do all this for you through The Messiah. You believe that promise. You confess your sins, and give yourself to God. You will to serve Him. Just as surely as you do this, God will fulfill His word to you. If you believe the promise—believe that you are forgiven and cleansed—God supplies the fact; you are made whole, just as The Messiah gave the paralytic power to walk when the man believed that he was healed. It is so if you believe it.

Do not wait to feel that you are made whole, but say, I believe it; it is so, not because I feel it, but because God has promised. The Redeemer says, what things soever ye desire, when ye pray, believe that ye receive them, and ye shall have them. There is a condition to this promise—that we pray according to the will of God. But it is the will of God to cleanse us from sin, to make us His children, and to enable us to live a holy life. So we may ask for these blessings, and believe that we receive them, and thank God that we *have* received them. It is our privilege to go to The Redeemer and be cleansed, and to stand before the law without shame or remorse.

Through this simple act of believing God, the Holy Spirit has begotten a new life in your heart. You are as a child born into the family of God, and He loves you as He loves His Son.

Now that you have given yourself to The Redeemer, do not draw back, do not take yourself away from Him, but day by day say, I am The Messiah's; I have given myself to Him; and ask Him to give you His Spirit, and keep you by His grace. As it is by giving yourself to God, and believing Him, that you become His child, so you are to live in Him.

Some seem to feel that they must be on probation, and must prove to the Lord that they are reformed, before they can claim His blessing. But they may claim the blessing of God even now. They must have His grace, the Spirit of The Messiah, to help their infirmities, or they cannot resist evil. The Redeemer loves to have us come to Him just as we are, sinful, helpless, dependent. We may come with all our weakness, our folly, our sinfulness, and fall at His feet in penitence. It is His glory to encircle us in the arms of His love, and to bind up our wounds, to cleanse us from all impurity.

Here is where thousands fail: they do not believe that The Redeemer pardons them personally, individually. They do not take God at His word. It is the privilege of all who comply with the conditions to know for themselves that pardon is freely extended for every sin. Put away the suspicion that God's promises are not meant for you. They are for every repentant transgressor. Strength and grace have been provided through The Messiah to be brought by ministering angels to every believing soul. None are so sinful that they cannot find strength, purity, and righteousness in The Redeemer, who died for them. He is waiting to strip them of their garments stained and polluted with sin, and to put upon them the white robes of righteousness; He bids them live and not die.

God does not deal with us as finite men deal with one another. His thoughts are thoughts of mercy, love, and tenderest compassion. He says, "Let the wicked forsake his way, and the unrighteous man his thoughts: and let him return unto the Lord, and He will have mercy upon him; and to our God, for He will abundantly pardon." "I have blotted out, as a thick cloud, thy transgression, and, as a cloud, thy sins." Isaiah 55:7; 44:22.

"I have no pleasure in the death of him that dieth, saith the Lord God: wherefore turn yourselves, and live ye." Ezekiel 18:32. Satan is ready to steal away the blessed assurances of God. He desires to take every glimmer of hope and every ray of light from the soul; but you must not permit him to do this. Do not give ear to the tempter, but say: The Redeemer has died that I might live. He loves me, and wills not that I should perish. I have a compassionate heavenly Father; and although I have abused His love, though the blessings He has given me have been squandered, I will arise, and go to my Father, and say, I have sinned against heaven, and before Thee, and am no more worthy to be called Thy son: make me as one of Thy hired servants. The parable tells you how the wanderer will be received: When he was yet a great way off, his father saw him, and had compassion, and ran, and fell on his neck, and kissed him.

But even this parable, tender and touching as it is, comes short of expressing the infinite compassion of the heavenly Father. The Lord declares by His prophet, "I have loved thee with an everlasting love: therefore with loving—kindness have I drawn thee." Jeremiah 31:3. While the sinner is yet far from the Father's house, wasting his substance in a strange country, the Father's heart is yearning over him; and every longing awakened in the soul to return to God, is but the tender pleading of His Spirit, wooing, entreating, drawing the wanderer to his Father's heart of love.

With the rich promises of the Bible before you, can you give place to doubt? Can you believe that when the poor sinner longs to return, longs to forsake his sins, the Lord sternly withholds him from coming to His feet in repentance? Away with such thoughts! Nothing can hurt your own soul more than to entertain such a conception of our heavenly Father. He hates sin, but He loves the sinner, and He gave Himself in the person of The Messiah, that all who would might be saved, and have eternal blessedness in the kingdom of glory. What stronger or more tender language could have been employed than He has chosen in which to express His love toward us? He declares, "Can a woman forget her sucking child, that she should not have compassion on the son of her womb? Yea, they may forget, yet will I not forget thee." Isaiah 49:15.

Look up, you that are doubting and trembling; for The Redeemer lives to make intercession for us. Thank God for the gift of His dear Son, and pray that He may not have died for you in vain. The Spirit invites you today. Come with your whole heart to The Redeemer, and you may claim His blessing.

As you read the promises, remember they are the expression of unutterable love and pity. The great heart of Infinite Love is drawn toward the sinner with boundless compassion. We have redemption through His blood, the forgiveness of sins. Yes, only believe that God is your helper. He wants to restore His moral image in man. As you draw near to Him with confession and repentance, He will draw near to you with mercy and forgiveness.

CHAPTER 7

The Acid Test

IF ANY MAN be in The Messiah, he is a new creature: old things are passed away; behold, all things are become new. Like the wind, which is invisible, yet the effects of which are plainly seen and felt, is the Spirit of God in its work upon the human heart. That regenerating power, which no human eye can see, begets a new life in the soul; it creates a new being in the image of God. While the work of the Spirit is silent and imperceptible, its effects are manifest. If the heart has been renewed by the Spirit of God, the life will bear witness to the fact. While we cannot do anything to change our hearts, or to bring ourselves into harmony with God; while we must not trust at all to ourselves or our good works, our lives will reveal whether the grace of God is dwelling within us. A change will be seen in the character, the habits, the pursuits. The contrast will be clear and decided between what they have been and what they are. The character is revealed, not by occasional good deeds and occasional misdeeds, but by the tendency of the habitual words and acts.

It is true that there may be an outward correctness of deportment without the renewing power of The Messiah. The love of influence and the desire for the esteem of others may produce a well-ordered life. Self-respect may lead us to avoid the appearance of evil. A selfish heart may perform generous actions. By what means, then, shall we determine whose side we are on?

Who has the heart? With whom are our thoughts? Of whom do we love to converse? Who has our warmest affections and our best energies? If we are The Messiah's, our thoughts are with Him, and our sweetest thoughts are of Him. All we have and are is consecrated to Him. We long to bear His image, breathe His spirit, do His will, and please Him in all things.

Those who become new creatures in The Messiah Redeemer will bring forth the fruits of the Spirit— love, joy, peace, long-suffering, gentleness, goodness, faith, meekness, temperance. They will no longer fashion themselves according

34

to the former lusts, but by the faith of The Messiah they will follow in His steps, reflect His character, and purify themselves even as He is pure. The things they once hated, they now love; and the things they once loved, they hate. The proud and self-assertive become meek and lowly in heart. The vain and supercilious become serious and unobtrusive. The drunken become sober, and the profligate pure. The vain customs and fashions of the world are laid aside. Believers will seek not the outward adorning, but the hidden man of the heart, in that which is not corruptible, even the ornament of a meek and quiet spirit.

There is no evidence of genuine repentance, unless it works reformation. If he restore the pledge, give again that he had robbed, confess his sins, and love God and his fellow men, the sinner may be sure that he has passed from death unto life.

When, as erring, sinful beings, we come to The Messiah and become partakers of His pardoning grace, love springs up in the heart. Every burden is light; for the yoke that The Messiah imposes is easy. Duty becomes a delight, and sacrifice a pleasure. The path that seemed shrouded in darkness, becomes bright with beams from the Sun of Righteousness.

The loveliness of the character of The Messiah will be seen in His followers. It was His delight to do the will of God. Love to God, zeal for His glory, was the controlling power in our Saviour's life. Love beautified and ennobled all His actions. Love is of God. The unconsecrated heart cannot originate or produce it. It is found only in the heart where The Redeemer reigns. In the heart renewed by divine grace, love is the principle of action. It modifies the character, governs the impulses, controls the passions, subdues enmity, and ennobles the affections. This love, cherished in the soul, sweetens the life, and sheds a refining influence on all around.

There are two errors against which the children of God—particularly those who have just come to trust in His grace—especially need to guard. The first, already dwelt upon, is that of looking to their own works, trusting to anything they can do, to bring themselves into harmony with God. He who is trying to become holy by his own works in keeping the law, is attempting an impossibility. All that man can do without The Messiah is polluted with selfishness and sin. It is the grace of The Messiah alone, through faith, that can make us holy.

The opposite and no less dangerous error is, that belief in The Messiah releases men from keeping the law of God; that since by faith alone we become partakers of the grace of The Messiah, our works have nothing to do with our redemption.

But notice here that obedience is not a mere outward compliance, but the service of love. The law of God is an expression of His very nature; it is an embodiment of the great principle of love, and hence is the foundation of His government in heaven and earth. If our hearts are renewed in the likeness of God, if the divine love is implanted in the soul, will not the law of God be carried out in the life? When the principle of love is implanted in the heart, when man is renewed after the image of Him that created him, the new covenant promise is fulfilled, "I will put My laws in their inward parts, and write it in their hearts; and will be their God, and they shall be my people." Jeremiah 31:33. And if the law is written in the heart, will it not shape the life? Obedience— the service and allegiance of love—is the true sign of discipleship. Instead of releasing man from obedience, it is faith, and faith only, that makes us partakers of the grace of The Messiah, which enables us to render obedience.

We do not earn salvation by our obedience; for salvation is the free gift of God, to be received by faith. But obedience is the fruit of faith. Here is the true test. If we abide in The Messiah, if the love of God dwells in us, our feelings, our thoughts, our purposes, our actions, will be in harmony with the will of God as expressed in the precepts of His holy law. Little children, let no man deceive you: he that doeth righteousness is righteous, even as He is righteous. Righteousness is defined by the standard of God's holy law, as expressed in the ten commandments given on Sinai.

That so-called faith in The Messiah which professes to release men from the obligation of obedience to God, is not faith, but presumption. By grace are ye saved through faith. But faith, if it hath not works, is dead. The Redeemer said of Himself before He came to earth, "I delight to do Thy will, O My God; yea, Thy law is within My heart." Psalm 40:8.

The condition of eternal life is now just what it always has been—just what it was in Paradise before the fall of our first parents—perfect obedience to the law of God, perfect righteousness. If eternal life were granted on any condition short of this, then the happiness of the whole universe would be imperiled. The way would be open for sin, with all its train of woe and misery, to be immortalized.

It was possible for Adam, before the fall, to form a righteous character by obedience to God's law. But he failed to do this, and because of his sin our natures are fallen, and we cannot make ourselves righteous. Since we are sinful, unholy, we cannot perfectly obey the holy law. We have no righteousness of our own with which to meet the claims of the law of God. But The Messiah has made a way of escape for us. He lived on earth amid trials and temptations such as we have to meet. He lived a sinless life. He died for us, and now He offers to take our sins and give us His righteousness. If you give yourself to Him, and accept Him as your Saviour, then, sinful as your life may have been, for His sake you are accounted righteous. The Messiah's character stands in place of your character, and you are accepted before God just as if you had not sinned.

More than this, The Messiah changes the heart. He abides in your heart by faith. You are to maintain this connection with The Messiah by faith and the continual surrender of your will to Him; and so long as you do this, He will work in you to will and to do according to His good pleasure. So you may say, the life which I now live in the flesh I live by the faith of the Son of God, who loved me, and gave Himself for me. Then with The Messiah working in you, you will manifest the same spirit and do the same good works—works of righteousness, obedience.

So we have nothing in ourselves of which to boast. We have no ground for self-exaltation. Our only ground of hope is in the righteousness of The Messiah imputed to us, and in that wrought by His Spirit working in and through us.

When we speak of faith, there is a distinction that should be borne in mind. There is a kind of belief that is wholly distinct from faith. The existence and power of God, the truth of His Word, are facts that even Satan and his hosts cannot at heart deny. The Bible says that the devils also believe and tremble; but this is not faith. Where there is not only a belief in God's Word, but a submission of the will to Him; where the heart is yielded to Him, the affections fixed upon Him, there is faith— faith that works by love, and purifies the soul. Through this faith the heart is renewed in the image of God. And the heart that in its unrenewed state is not subject to the law of God, neither indeed can be, now delights in its holy precepts, exclaiming with the psalmist, "O how love I Thy law! it is my meditation all the day." Psalm 119:97. And the righteousness of the law is fulfilled in us, who walk not after the flesh, but after the Spirit.

There are those who have known the pardoning love of The Messiah, and who really desire to be children of God, yet they realize that their character is imperfect, their life faulty, and they are ready to doubt whether their hearts have been renewed by the Holy Spirit. To such I would say, Do not draw back in despair. We shall often have to bow down and weep at the feet of The Redeemer because of our shortcomings and mistakes; but we are not to be discouraged. Even if we are overcome by the enemy, we are not cast off, not forsaken and rejected of God. No; The Messiah is at the right hand of God, who also makes intercession for us. Do not forget the words of The Messiah, The Father Himself loves you. He desires to restore you to Himself, to see His own purity and holiness reflected in you. And if you will but yield yourself to Him, He that hath begun a good work in you will carry it forward to the day of The Messiah Redeemer. Pray more fervently; believe more fully. As we come to distrust our own power, let us trust the power of our Redeemer, and we shall praise Him who is the health of our countenance.

The closer you come to The Redeemer, the more faulty you will appear in your own eyes; for your vision will be clearer, and your imperfections will be seen in broad and distinct contrast to His perfect nature. This is evidence that Satan's delusions have lost their power; that the vivifying influence of the Spirit of God is arousing you.

No deep-seated love for The Redeemer can dwell in the heart that does not realize its own sinfulness. The soul that is transformed by the grace of The Messiah will admire His divine character; but if we do not see our own moral deformity, it is unmistakable evidence that we have not had a view of the beauty and excellence of The Messiah.

The less we see to esteem in ourselves, the more we shall see to esteem in the infinite purity and loveliness of our Saviour. A view of our sinfulness drives us to Him who can pardon; and when the soul, realizing its helplessness, reaches out after The Messiah, He will reveal Himself in power. The more our sense of need drives us to Him and to the Word of God, the more exalted views we shall have of His character, and the more fully we shall reflect His image.

CHAPTER 8

Measuring Up

THE CHANGE OF HEART by which we become children of God is in the Bible spoken of as birth. Again, it is compared to the germination of the good seed sown by the husbandman. In like manner those who have just given their life to The Messiah are, as newborn babes, to grow up to the stature of men and women in The Messiah Redeemer. Or like the good seed sown in the field, they are to grow up and bring forth fruit. Isaiah says that they shall "be called trees of righteousness, the planting of the Lord, that He might be glorified." Isaiah 61:3. So from natural life, illustrations are drawn, to help us better to understand the mysterious truths of spiritual life.

Not all the wisdom and skill of man can produce life in the smallest object in nature. It is only through the life which God Himself has imparted, that either plant or animal can live. So it is only through the life from God that spiritual life is begotten in the hearts of men. Unless a man is born from above, he cannot become a partaker of the life which The Messiah came to give.

As with life, so it is with growth. It is God who brings the bud to bloom and the flower to fruit. It is by His power that the seed develops, first the blade, then the ear, after that the full corn in the ear. And the prophet Hosea says of Israel, that "he shall grow as the lily." "They shall revive as the corn, and grow as the vine." Hosea 14:5, 7. The plants and flowers grow not by their own care or anxiety or effort, but by receiving that which God has furnished to minister to their life. The child cannot, by any anxiety or power of its own, add to its stature. No more can you, by anxiety or effort of yourself, secure spiritual growth. The plant, the child, grows by receiving from its surroundings that which ministers to its life—air, sunshine, and food. What these gifts of nature are to animal and plant, such is The Messiah to those who trust in Him. He is their "everlasting light," "a sun and shield." Isaiah 60:19; Psalm 84:11. He shall be as "the dew unto Israel." "He shall come down like rain upon the mown grass." Hosea 14:5; Psalm 72:6.

He is the living water, the bread of God which comes down from heaven, and gives life unto the world.

In the matchless gift of His Son, God has encircled the whole world with an atmosphere of grace as real as the air which circulates around the globe. All who choose to breathe this life-giving atmosphere will live, and grow up to the stature of men and women in The Messiah Redeemer.

As the flower turns to the sun, that the bright beams may aid in perfecting its beauty and symmetry, so should we turn to the Sun of Righteousness, that heaven's light may shine upon us, that our character may be developed into the likeness of The Messiah.

The Redeemer teaches the same thing when He says, Abide in Me, and I in you. As the branch cannot bear fruit of itself, except it abide in the vine; no more can ye, except ye abide in Me. Without Me ye can do nothing. You are just as dependent upon The Messiah, in order to live a holy life, as is the branch upon the parent stock for growth and fruitfulness. Apart from Him you have no life. You have no power to resist temptation or to grow in grace and holiness. Abiding in Him, you may flourish. Drawing your life from Him, you will not wither nor be fruitless. You will be like a tree planted by the rivers of water.

Many have an idea that they must do some part of the work alone. They have trusted in The Messiah for the forgiveness of sin, but now they seek by their own efforts to live aright. But every such effort must fail. The Redeemer says, Without Me ye can do nothing. Our growth in grace, our joy, our usefulness—all depend upon our union with The Messiah. It is by communion with Him, daily, hourly—by abiding in Him— that we are to grow in grace. He is not only the Author but the Finisher of our faith. It is The Messiah first and last and always. He is to be with us, not only at the beginning and the end of our course, but at every step of the way. David says, "I have set the Lord always before me: because He is at my right hand, I shall not be moved." Psalm 16:8.Do you ask, how am I to abide in The Messiah? — In the same way as you received Him at first. You gave yourself to God, to be His wholly, to serve and obey Him, and you took The Messiah as your Saviour. You could not yourself atone for your sins or change your heart; but having given yourself to God, you believed that He for The Messiah's sake did all this for you. By faith you became The Messiah's, and by faith you are to grow up in Him—by giving and taking. You are to give all—your heart, your will, your service—give yourself to Him to obey all His requirements; and you must take all—The Messiah, the fullness of all blessing, to abide in your heart, to be your strength, your righteousness, your everlasting helper—to give you power to obey.

Consecrate yourself to God in the morning; make this your very first work. Let your prayer be, "Take me, O Lord, as wholly Thine. I lay all my plans at Thy feet. Use me today in Thy service. Abide with me, and let all my work be wrought in Thee." This is a daily matter. Each morning consecrate yourself to God for that day. Surrender all your plans to Him, to be carried out or given up as His providence shall indicate. Thus day by day you may be giving your life into the hands of God, and thus your life will be molded more and more after the life of The Messiah.

A life in The Messiah is a life of restfulness. There may be no ecstasy of feeling, but there should be an abiding, peaceful trust. Your hope is not in yourself; it is in The Messiah. Your weakness is united to His strength, your ignorance to His wisdom, your frailty to His enduring might. So you are not to look to yourself, not to let the mind dwell upon self, but look to The Messiah. Let the mind dwell upon His love, upon the beauty, the perfection, of His character. The Messiah in His self-denial, The Messiah in His humiliation, The Messiah in His purity and holiness, The Messiah in His matchless love— this is the subject for the soul's contemplation. It is by loving Him, copying Him, depending wholly upon Him, that you are to be transformed into His likeness.

The Redeemer says, abide in Me. These words convey the idea of rest, stability, confidence. Again He invites, come unto Me, and I will give you rest. The words of the psalmist express the same thought: "Rest in the Lord, and wait patiently for Him." And Isaiah gives the assurance, "In quietness and confidence shall be your strength." Psalm 37:7; Isaiah 30:15. This rest is not found in inactivity; for in the Saviour's invitation the promise of rest is united with the call to labor. The heart that rests most fully upon The Messiah will be most earnest and active in labor for Him.

When the mind dwells upon self, it is turned away from The Messiah, the source of strength and life. Hence it is Satan's constant effort to keep the attention diverted from the

Saviour, and thus prevent the union and communion of the soul
with The Messiah. The pleasures of the world, life's cares and
perplexities and sorrows, the faults of others, or your own
faults and imperfections—to any or all of these he will seek to
divert the mind. Do not be misled by his devices. Many who
are really conscientious, and who desire to live for God, he too
often leads to dwell upon their own faults and weaknesses, and
thus by separating them from The Messiah, he hopes to gain
the victory. We should not make self the center, and indulge
anxiety and fear as to whether we shall be saved. All this turns
the soul away from the Source of our strength. Commit the
keeping of your soul to God, and trust in Him. Talk and think
of The Redeemer. Let self be lost in Him. Put away all doubt;
dismiss your fears. Say with Paul, I live; yet not I, but The
Messiah liveth in me: and the life which I now live in the flesh
I live by the faith of the Son of God, who loved me, and gave
Himself for me. Rest in God. He is able to keep that which
you have committed to Him. If you will leave yourself in His
hands, He will bring you off more than conqueror through Him
that has loved you.

When The Messiah took human nature upon Him, He
bound humanity to Himself by a tie of love that can never be
broken by any power save the choice of man himself. Satan
will constantly present allurements to induce us to break this
tie—to choose to separate ourselves from The Messiah. Here
is where we need to watch, to strive, to pray, that nothing may
entice us to choose another master; for we are always free to do
this. But let us keep our eyes fixed upon The Messiah, and He
will preserve us. Looking unto The Redeemer, we are safe.
Nothing can pluck us out of His hand. In constantly beholding
Him, we are changed into the same image from glory to glory,
even as by the Spirit of the Lord.

It was thus that the early disciples gained their likeness to
the dear Saviour. When those disciples heard the words of The
Redeemer, they felt their need of Him. They sought, they
found, they followed Him. They were with Him in the house,
at the table, in the closet, in the field. They were with Him as
pupils with a teacher, daily receiving from His lips lessons of
holy truth. They looked to Him, as servants to their master, to
learn their duty. They had the same battle with sin to fight.
They needed the same grace, in order to live a holy life.

Even John, the one who most fully reflected the likeness of the Saviour, did not naturally possess that loveliness of character. He was not only self-assertive and ambitious for honor, but impetuous, and resentful under injuries. But as the character of the Divine One was manifested to him, he saw his own deficiency, and was humbled by the knowledge. The strength and patience, the power and tenderness, the majesty and meekness, that he beheld in the daily life of The Messiah filled his soul with admiration and love. Day by day his heart was drawn out toward Him, until he lost sight of self in love for his Master. His resentful, ambitious temper was yielded to the molding power of The Messiah. The regenerating influence of the Holy Spirit renewed his heart. The power of the love of The Messiah wrought a transformation of character. This is the sure result of union with The Redeemer. When The Messiah abides in the heart, the whole nature is transformed. The Messiah's Spirit, His love, softens the heart, subdues the soul, and raises the thoughts and desires toward God and heaven.

When The Messiah ascended to heaven, the sense of His presence was still with His followers. It was a personal presence, full of love and light. The Redeemer, the Saviour, who had walked and talked and prayed with them, who had spoken hope and comfort to their hearts, had, while the message of peace was still upon His lips, been taken up from them into heaven, and the tones of His voice had come back to them, as the cloud of angels received Him. He had ascended to heaven in the form of humanity. They knew that He was before the throne of God, their Friend and Saviour still; that His sympathies were unchanged; that He was still identified with suffering humanity. He was presenting before God the merits of His own precious blood, showing His wounded hands and feet, in remembrance of the price He had paid for His redeemed. They knew that He had ascended to heaven to prepare places for them, and that He would come again, and take them to Himself.

As they met together, after the ascension, they were eager to present their requests to the Father in the name of The Redeemer. In solemn awe they bowed in prayer, repeating the assurance, what ever ye shall ask the Father in My name, He will give it you. From this point through the Spirit, The Messiah was to abide continually in the hearts of His children. Their union with Him was closer than when He was personally with them. The light, and love, and power of the indwelling

Messiah shone out through them, so that men, beholding, marveled; and they took knowledge of them, that they had been with The Redeemer.

All that The Messiah was to the disciples, He desires to be to His children today; for in that last prayer, with the little band of disciples gathered about Him, He said, neither pray I for you alone, but for them also which shall believe on Me through your word. The Redeemer prayed for us, and He asked that we might be one with Him, even as He is one with the Father. We shall work as He worked; we shall manifest the same spirit. And thus, loving Him and abiding in Him, we shall grow up into Him in all things, which is the head, even The Messiah.

CHAPTER 9

"Giving" Means Living

GOD IS THE SOURCE of life and light and joy to the universe. Like rays of light from the sun, like the streams of water bursting from a living spring, blessings flow out from Him to all His creatures. And wherever the life of God is in the hearts of men, it will flow out to others in love and blessing.

Our Saviour's joy was in the uplifting and redemption of fallen men. For this He counted not His life dear unto Himself, but endured the cross, despising the shame. So angels are ever engaged in working for the happiness of others. This is their joy. That which selfish hearts would regard as humiliating service, ministering to those who are wretched and in every way inferior in character and rank, is the work of sinless angels. The spirit of The Messiah's self-sacrificing love is the spirit that pervades heaven, and is the very essence of its bliss. This is the spirit that The Messiah's followers will possess, the work that they will do.

When the love of The Messiah is enshrined in the heart, like sweet fragrance it cannot be hidden. Its holy influence will be felt by all with whom we come in contact. The spirit of The Messiah in the heart is like a spring in the desert, flowing to refresh all, and making those who are ready to perish, eager to drink of the water of life.

Love to The Redeemer will be manifested in a desire to work as He worked, for the blessing and uplifting of humanity. It will lead to love, tenderness, and sympathy toward all the creatures of our heavenly Father's care.

The Saviour's life on earth was not a life of ease and devotion to Himself, but He toiled with persistent, earnest, untiring effort for the salvation of lost mankind. He followed the path of self-denial, and sought not to be released from arduous tasks, painful travels, and exhausting care and labor. This was the one great object of His life. Everything else was secondary and subservient. It was His meat and drink to do the will of God and to finish His work. Self and self-interest had no part in His labor.

45

So those who are the partakers of the grace of The Messiah will be ready to make any sacrifice, that others for whom He died may share the heavenly gift. They will do all they can to make the world better for their stay in it. This spirit is the sure outgrowth of a soul truly converted. No sooner does one come to The Messiah, than there is born in his heart a desire to make known to others what a precious friend he has found in The Redeemer; the saving and sanctifying truth cannot be shut up in his heart. If we are clothed with the righteousness of The Messiah, and are filled with the joy of His indwelling Spirit, we shall not be able to hold our peace. If we have tasted and seen that the Lord is good, we shall have something to tell. Like Philip when he found the Saviour, we shall invite others into His presence. We shall seek to present to them the attractions of The Messiah, and the unseen realities of the world to come. There will be an intensity of desire to follow in the path that The Redeemer trod. There will be an earnest longing that those around us may behold the Lamb of God, which taketh away the sin of the world.

And the effort to bless others will react in blessings upon ourselves. This was the purpose of God in giving us a part to act in the plan of redemption. He has granted men the privilege of becoming partakers of the divine nature, and, in their turn, of diffusing blessings to their fellow men. This is the highest honor, the greatest joy, that it is possible for God to bestow upon men. Those who thus become participants in labors of love are brought nearest to their Creator.

God might have committed the message of good news, and all the work of loving ministry, to the heavenly angels. He might have employed other means for accomplishing His purpose. But in His infinite love He chose to make us co-workers with Himself, with The Messiah and the angels, that we might share the blessing, the joy, the spiritual uplifting, which results from this unselfish ministry.

We are brought into sympathy with The Messiah through the fellowship of His sufferings. Every act of self-sacrifice for the good of others strengthens the spirit of beneficence in the giver's heart, allying him more closely to The Redeemer of the world, who was rich, yet for your sakes became poor, that ye through His poverty might be rich. And it is only as we thus fulfill the divine purpose in our creation, that life can be a blessing to us.

If you will go to work as The Messiah has designed for you, you will feel the need of a deeper experience and a greater knowledge in divine things, and will hunger and thirst after righteousness. You will plead with God, and your faith will be strengthened, and your soul will drink deeper drafts at the well of salvation. Encountering opposition and trials will drive you to the Bible and prayer. You will grow in grace and the knowledge of The Messiah, and will develop a rich experience.

The spirit of unselfish labor for others gives depth, stability, and Christlike loveliness to the character, and brings peace and happiness to its possessor. The aspirations are elevated. There is no room for sloth or selfishness. Those who thus exercise the Believer graces will grow, and will become strong to work for God. They will have clear spiritual perceptions, a steady, growing faith, and an increased power in prayer. The Spirit of God, moving upon their spirit, calls forth the sacred harmonies of the soul, in answer to the divine touch. Those who thus devote themselves to unselfish effort for the good of others, are most surely working out their own salvation.

The only way to grow in grace is to be disinterestedly doing the very work which The Messiah has enjoined upon us—to engage, to the extent of our ability, in helping and blessing those who need the help we can give them. Strength comes by exercise; activity is the very condition of life. Those who endeavor to maintain The Believers' life by passively accepting the blessings that come through the means of grace, and doing nothing for The Messiah, are simply trying to live by eating without working. And in the spiritual as in the natural world, this always results in degeneration and decay. A man who would refuse to exercise his limbs would soon lose all power to use them. Thus the Believer who will not exercise his God-given powers, not only fails to grow up into The Messiah, but he loses the strength that he already had.

The house of God is the Messiah's appointed agency for the salvation of men. Its mission is to carry the good news to the world. And the obligation rests upon all Believers. Every one, to the extent of his talent and opportunity, is to fulfill The Saviour's commission. The love of The Messiah, revealed to us, makes us debtors to all who know Him not. God has given us light, not for ourselves alone, but to shed upon them.

We need not go to heathen lands, or even leave the narrow circle of the home, if it is there that our duty lies, in order to work for The Messiah. We can do this in the home circle, in the house of God, among those with whom we associate, and with whom we do business.

The greater part of our Saviour's life on earth was spent in patient toil in the carpenter's shop at Nazareth. Ministering angels attended the Lord of life as He walked side by side with peasants and laborers, unrecognized and unhonored. He was as faithfully fulfilling His mission while working at His humble trade as when He healed the sick or walked upon the storm-tossed waves of Galilee. So, in the humblest duties and lowliest positions of life, we may walk and work with The Redeemer.

The businessman may conduct his business in a way that will glorify his Master because of his fidelity. If he is a true follower of The Messiah, he will carry his religion into everything that is done, and reveal to men the spirit of The Messiah. The mechanic may be a diligent and faithful representative of Him who toiled in the lowly walks of life among the hills of Galilee. Everyone who names the name of The Messiah should so work that others, by seeing his good works, may be led to glorify their Creator and Redeemer.

Many have excused themselves from rendering their gifts to the service of The Messiah, because others were possessed of superior endowments and advantages. The opinion has prevailed that only those who are especially talented are required to consecrate their abilities to the service of God. It has come to be understood by many that talents are given to only a certain favored class, to the exclusion of others, who of course, are not called upon to share in the toils or the rewards. But it is not so represented in the parable. When the master of the house called his servants, he gave to every man his work.

With a loving spirit we may perform life's humblest duties as to the Lord. If the love of God is in the heart, it will be manifested in the life. The sweet savor of The Messiah will surround us, and our influence will elevate and bless.

You are not to wait for great occasions or to expect extraordinary abilities before you go to work for God. You need not have a thought of what the world will think of you. If your daily life is a testimony to the purity and sincerity of your faith, and others are convinced that you desire to benefit them, your efforts will not be wholly lost.

The humblest and poorest of the disciples of The Redeemer can be a blessing to others. They may not realize that they are doing any special good, but by their unconscious influence they may start waves of blessing that will widen and deepen, and the blessed results they may never know until the day of final reward. They do not feel or know that they are doing anything great. They are not required to weary themselves with anxiety about success. They have only to go forward quietly, doing faithfully the work that God's providence assigns, and their life will not be in vain. Their own souls will be growing more and more into the likeness of The Messiah; they are workers together with God in this life, and are thus fitting for the higher work and the unshadowed joy of the life to come.

CHAPTER 10

Listen to God

MANY ARE THE WAYS in which God is seeking to make Himself known to us and bring us into communion with Him. Nature speaks to our senses without ceasing. The open heart will be impressed with the love and glory of God as revealed through the works of His hands. The listening ear can hear and understand the communications of God through the things of nature. The green fields, the lofty trees, the buds and flowers, the passing cloud, the falling rain, the babbling brook, the glories of the heavens, speak to our hearts, and invite us to become acquainted with Him who made them all.

Our Saviour bound up His precious lessons with the things of nature. The trees, the birds, the flowers of the valleys, the hills, the lakes, and the beautiful heavens, as well as the incidents and surroundings of daily life, were all linked with the words of truth, that His lessons might thus be often recalled to mind, even amid the busy cares of man's life of toil.

God would have His children appreciate His works, and delight in the simple, quiet beauty with which He has adorned our earthly home. He is a lover of the beautiful, and above all that is outwardly attractive He loves beauty of character; He would have us cultivate purity and simplicity, the quiet graces of the flowers.

If we will but listen, God's created works will teach us precious lessons of obedience and trust. From the stars that in their trackless courses through space follow from age to age their appointed path, down to the minutest atom, the things of nature obey the Creator's will. And God cares for everything and sustains everything that He has created. He who upholds the unnumbered worlds throughout immensity, at the same time cares for the wants of the little brown sparrow that sings its humble song without fear. When men go forth to their daily toil, as when they engage in prayer; when they lie down at night, and when they rise in the morning; when the rich man feasts in his palace, or when the poor man gathers his children about the scanty board, each is tenderly watched by the heavenly Father. No tears are shed that God does not notice. There is no smile that He does not mark.

If we would but fully believe this, all undue anxieties would be dismissed. Our lives would not be so filled with disappointment as now; for everything, whether great or small, would be left in the hands of God, who is not perplexed by the multiplicity of cares, or overwhelmed by their weight. We should then enjoy a rest of soul to which many have long been strangers.

As your senses delight in the attractive loveliness of the earth, think of the world that is to come, that shall never know the blight of sin and death; where the face of nature will no more wear the shadow of the curse. Let your imagination picture the home of the saved, and remember that it will be more glorious than your brightest imagination can portray. In the varied gifts of God in nature we see but the faintest gleaming of His glory. It is written, "Eye hath not seen, nor ear heard, neither have entered into the heart of man, the things which God hath prepared for them that love Him." Isaiah 64:4

The poet and the naturalist have many things to say about nature, but it is the Believer who enjoys the beauty of the earth with the highest appreciation, because he recognizes his Father's handiwork, and perceives His love in flower and shrub and tree. No one can fully appreciate the significance of hill and vale, river and sea, who does not look upon them as an expression of God's love to man.

God speaks to us through His providential workings, and through the influence of His Spirit upon the heart. In our circumstances and surroundings, in the changes daily taking place around us, we may find precious lessons, if our hearts are but open to discern them. The psalmist, tracing the work of God's providence, says, "The earth is full of the goodness of the Lord." Psalm 33:5. "Whoso is wise, and will observe these things, even they shall understand the loving-kindness of the Lord." Psalm 107:43.

God speaks to us in His Word. Here we have in clearer lines the revelation of His character, of His dealings with men, and the great work of redemption. Here is open before us the history of Patriarchs and Prophets and other Holy men of old. They were men subject to like passions as we are. We see how they struggled through discouragements like our own, how they fell under temptation as we have done, and yet took heart again and conquered through the grace of God; and, beholding, we are encouraged in our striving after righteousness. As we read of the precious experiences granted them, of the light and love and blessing it was theirs to enjoy, and of the work they wrought through the grace given them, the spirit that inspired them kindles a flame of holy emulation in our hearts, and a desire to be like them in character—like them to walk with God.

The Holy Scriptures tell of The Messiah. From the first record of creation to the closing promise, I come quickly, we are reading of His works and listening to His voice. If you would become acquainted with The Saviour, study the Holy Scriptures. Fill the whole heart with the words of God. They are the living water, quenching your burning thirst. They are the living bread from heaven. Our bodies are built up from what we eat and drink; and as in the natural economy, so in the spiritual economy: it is what we meditate upon that will give tone and strength to our spiritual nature.

The theme of redemption is one that the angels desire to look into; it will be the science and the song of the redeemed throughout the ceaseless ages of eternity. Is it not worthy of careful thought and study now? The infinite mercy and love of The Redeemer, the sacrifice made in our behalf, call for the most serious and solemn reflection. We should dwell upon the character of our dear Redeemer and Intercessor. We should meditate upon the mission of Him who came to save His people from their sins. As we thus contemplate heavenly themes, our faith and love will grow stronger, and our prayers will be more and more acceptable to God, because they will be more and more mixed with faith and love. They will be intelligent and fervent. There will be more constant confidence in The Redeemer, and a daily, living experience in His power to save to the uttermost all that come unto God by Him.

As we meditate upon the perfections of the Saviour, we shall desire to be wholly transformed, and renewed in the image of His purity. There will be a hungering and thirsting of soul to become like Him whom we adore. The more our thoughts are upon The Messiah, the more we shall speak of Him to others, and represent Him to the world.

The Bible was not written for the scholar alone; on the contrary, it was designed for the common people. The great truths necessary for salvation are made as clear as noonday; and none will mistake and lose their way except those who follow their own judgment instead of the plainly revealed will of God.

We should not take the testimony of any man as to what the Scriptures teach, but should study the words of God for ourselves. If we allow others to do our thinking, we shall have crippled energies and contracted abilities. The noble powers of the mind may be so dwarfed by lack of exercise on themes worthy of their concentration as to lose their ability to grasp the deep meaning of the Word of God. The mind will enlarge if it is employed in tracing out the relation of the subjects of the Bible, comparing scripture with scripture, and spiritual things with spiritual.

There is nothing more calculated to strengthen the intellect than the study of the Scriptures. No other book is so potent to elevate the thoughts, to give vigor to the faculties, as the broad, ennobling truths of the Bible. If God's Word were studied as it should be, men would have a breadth of mind, a nobility of character, and a stability of purpose rarely seen in these times.

But there is but little benefit derived from a hasty reading of the Scriptures. One may read the whole Bible through, and yet fail to see its beauty or comprehend its deep and hidden meaning. One passage studied until its significance is clear to the mind, and its relation to the plan of salvation is evident, is of more value than the perusal of many chapters with no definite purpose in view and no positive instruction gained. Keep your Bible with you. As you have opportunity, read it; fix the texts in your memory. Even while you are walking the streets, you may read a passage, and meditate upon it, thus fixing it in the mind.

We cannot obtain wisdom without earnest attention and prayerful study. Some portions of Scripture are indeed too plain to be misunderstood; but there are others whose meaning does not lie on the surface, to be seen at a glance. Scripture must be compared with scripture. There must be careful research and prayerful reflection. And such study will be richly repaid. As the miner discovers veins of precious metal concealed beneath the surface of the earth, so will he who perseveringly searches the Word of God as for hid treasure, find truths of the greatest value, which are concealed from the view of the careless seeker. The words of inspiration, pondered in the heart, will be as streams flowing from the fountain of life.

Never should the Bible be studied without prayer. Before opening its pages we should ask for the enlightenment of the Holy Spirit, and it will be given. The Redeemer will see us also in the secret places of prayer, if we will seek Him for light that we may know what is truth. Angels from the world of light will be with those who in humility of heart seek for divine guidance.

The Holy Spirit exalts and glorifies the Saviour. It is His office to present The Messiah, the purity of His righteousness, and the great salvation that we have through Him. The Spirit of truth is the only effectual teacher of divine truth. How must God esteem the human race, since He gave His Son to die for them, and appoints His Spirit to be man's teacher and continual guide!

CHAPTER 11

Hidden Treasure

THROUGH NATURE AND revelation, through His providence, and by the influence of His Spirit, God speaks to us. But these are not enough; we need also to pour out our hearts to Him. In order to have spiritual life and energy, we must have actual communion with our heavenly Father. Our minds may be drawn out toward Him; we may meditate upon His works, His mercies, His blessings; but this is not, in the fullest sense, communing with Him. In order to commune with God, we must have something to say to Him concerning our actual life.

Prayer is the opening of the heart to God as to a friend. Not that it is necessary, in order to make known to God what we are, but in order to enable us to receive Him. Prayer does not bring God down to us, but brings us up to Him.

When The Redeemer was upon the earth, He taught His disciples how to pray. He directed them to present their daily needs before God, and to cast all their care upon Him. And the assurance He gave them that their petitions should be heard, is assurance also to us.

The Redeemer Himself, while He dwelt among men, was often in prayer. Our Saviour identified Himself with our needs and weakness, in that He became a suppliant, a petitioner, seeking from His Father fresh supplies of strength, that He might come forth braced for duty and trial. He is our example in all things. He is a brother in our infirmities, in all points tempted like as we are; but as the Sinless One His nature recoiled from evil; He endured struggles and torture of soul in a world of sin. His humanity made prayer a necessity and a privilege. He found comfort and joy in communion with His Father. And if the Saviour of men, The Messiah, felt the need of prayer, how much more should feeble, sinful mortals feel the necessity of fervent, constant prayer.

Our heavenly Father waits to bestow upon us the fullness of His blessing. It is our privilege to drink largely at the fountain of boundless love. What a wonder it is that we pray so little! God is ready and willing to hear the sincere prayer of the humblest of His children, and yet there is much manifest reluctance on our part to make known our wants to God. What can the angels of heaven think of poor helpless human beings, who are subject to temptation, when God's heart of infinite love yearns toward them, ready to give them more than they can ask or think, and yet they pray so little, and have so little faith? The angels love to bow before God; they love to be near Him. They regard communion with God as their highest joy; and yet the children of earth, who need so much the help that God only can give, seem satisfied to walk without the light of His Spirit, the companionship of His presence.

The darkness of the evil one encloses those who neglect to pray. The whispered temptations of the enemy entice them to sin; and it is all because they do not make use of the privileges that God has given them in the divine appointment of prayer. Why should the sons and daughters of God be reluctant to pray, when prayer is the key in the hand of faith to unlock heaven's storehouse, where are treasured the boundless resources of Omnipotence. Without unceasing prayer and diligent watching, we are in danger of growing careless and of deviating from the right path. The adversary seeks continually to obstruct the way to the mercy seat, that we may not by earnest supplication and faith obtain grace and power to resist temptation.

There are certain conditions upon which we may expect that God will hear and answer our prayers. One of the first of these is that we feel our need of help from Him. He has promised, "I will pour water upon him that is thirsty, and floods upon the dry ground." Isaiah 44:3. Those who hunger and thirst after righteousness, who long after God, may be sure that they will be filled. The heart must be open to the Spirit's influence, or God's blessing cannot be received. Our great need is itself an argument, and pleads most eloquently in our behalf. But the Lord is to be sought unto to do these things for us.

If we regard iniquity in our hearts, if we cling to any known sin, the Lord will not hear us; but the prayer of the penitent, contrite soul is always accepted. When all known wrongs are righted, we may believe that God will answer our petitions. Our own merit will never commend us to the favor of God; it is the worthiness of The Redeemer that will save us, His blood that will cleanse us; yet we have a work to do in complying with the conditions of acceptance.

The assurance is broad and unlimited, and He is faithful who has promised. When we do not receive the very things we ask for, at the time we ask, we are still to believe that the Lord hears, and that He will answer our prayers. We are so erring and shortsighted that we sometimes ask for things that would not be a blessing to us, and our heavenly Father in love answers our prayers by giving us that which will be for our highest good—that which we ourselves would desire if with vision divinely enlightened we could see all things as they really are. When our prayers seem not to be answered, we are to cling to the promise; for the time of answering will surely come, and we shall receive the blessing we need most. But to claim that prayer will always be answered in the very way and for the particular thing that we desire, is presumption. God is too wise to err, and too good to withhold any good thing from them that walk uprightly. Then do not fear to trust Him, even though you do not see the immediate answer to your prayers. Rely upon His sure promise, ask, and it shall be given you.

If we take counsel with our doubts and fears, or try to solve everything that we cannot see clearly, before we have faith, perplexities will only increase and deepen. But if we come to God, feeling helpless and dependent, as we really are, and in humble, trusting faith make known our wants to Him whose knowledge is infinite, who sees everything in creation, and who governs everything by His will and word, He can and will attend to our cry, and will let light shine into our hearts. Through sincere prayer we are brought into connection with the mind of the Infinite. We may have no remarkable evidence at the time that the face of our Redeemer is bending over us in compassion and love; but this is even so. We may not feel His visible touch, but His hand is upon us in love and pitying tenderness.

When we come to ask mercy and blessing from God, we should have a spirit of love and forgiveness in our own hearts. How can we pray, forgive us our debts, as we forgive our debtors, and yet indulge an unforgiving spirit? If we expect our own prayers to be heard, we must forgive others in the same manner, and to the same extent, as we hope to be forgiven. Perseverance in prayer has been made a condition of receiving. We must pray always, if we would grow in faith and experience. We are to be instant in prayer, to continue in prayer, and watch in the same with thanksgiving. Unceasing prayer is the unbroken union of the soul with God, so that life from God flows into our life; and from our life, purity and holiness flow back to God.

There is necessity for diligence in prayer; let nothing hinder you. Make every effort to keep open the communion between The Redeemer and your own soul. Seek every opportunity to go where prayer is wont to be made. Those who are really seeking for communion with God, will be seen in the prayer meeting, faithful to do their duty, and earnest and anxious to reap all the benefits they can gain. They will improve every opportunity of placing themselves where they can receive the rays of light from heaven.

We should pray in the family circle; and above all we must not neglect secret prayer; for this is the life of the soul. It is impossible for the soul to flourish while prayer is neglected. Family or public prayer alone is not sufficient. In solitude let the soul be laid open to the inspecting eye of God. Secret prayer is to be heard only by the prayer-hearing God. No curious ear is to receive the burden of such petitions. In secret prayer the soul is free from surrounding influences, free from excitement. Calmly, yet fervently, will it reach out after God. Sweet and abiding will be the influence emanating from Him who seeth in secret, whose ear is open to hear the prayer arising from the heart. By calm, simple faith, the soul holds communion with God, and gathers to itself rays of divine light to strengthen and sustain it in the conflict with Satan. God is our tower of strength.

Pray in your closet; and as you go about your daily labor, let your heart be often uplifted to God. It was thus that Enoch walked with God. These silent prayers rise like precious incense before the throne of grace. Satan cannot overcome him whose heart is thus stayed upon God.

There is no time or place in which it is inappropriate to offer up a petition to God. There is nothing that can prevent us from lifting up our hearts in the spirit of earnest prayer. In the crowds of the street, in the midst of a business engagement, we may send up a petition to God, and plead for divine guidance, as did Nehemiah when he made his request before King Artaxerxes. A closet of communion may be found wherever we are. We should have the door of the heart open continually, and our invitation going up that The Redeemer may come and abide as a heavenly guest in the soul.

Although there may be a tainted, corrupted atmosphere around us, we need not breathe its miasma, but may live in the pure air of heaven. We may close every door to impure imaginings and unholy thoughts by lifting the soul into the presence of God through sincere prayer. Those whose hearts are open to receive the support and blessing of God will walk in a holier atmosphere than that of earth, and will have constant communion with heaven.

We need to have more distinct views of The Redeemer, and a fuller comprehension of the value of eternal realities. The beauty of holiness is to fill the hearts of God's children; and that this may be accomplished, we should seek for divine disclosures of heavenly things.

Let the soul be drawn out and upward, that God may grant us a breath of the heavenly atmosphere. We may keep so near to God that in every unexpected trial our thoughts will turn to Him as naturally as the flower turns to the sun.

Keep your wants, your joys, your sorrows, your cares, and your fears, before God. You cannot burden Him; you cannot weary Him. He who numbers the hairs of your head is not indifferent to the wants of His children. The Lord is very pitiful, and of tender mercy. His heart of love is touched by our sorrows, and even by our utterance of them. Take to Him everything that perplexes the mind. Nothing is too great for Him to bear, for He holds up worlds, He rules over all the affairs of the universe. Nothing that in any way concerns our peace is too small for Him to notice. There is no chapter in our experience too dark for Him to read; there is no perplexity too difficult for Him to unravel. No calamity can befall the least of His children, no anxiety harass the soul, no joy cheer, no sincere prayer escape the lips, of which our heavenly Father is unobservant, or in which He takes no immediate interest. "He healeth the broken in heart, and bindeth up their wounds." Psalm 147:3. The relations between God and each soul are as distinct and full as though there were not another soul upon the earth to share His watchcare, not another soul for whom He gave His beloved Son.

To pray in the name of The Redeemer is something more than a mere mention of that name at the beginning and the ending of a prayer. It is to pray in the mind and spirit of The

Redeemer, while we believe His promises, rely upon His grace and work His works.

God does not mean that any of us should become hermits or monks, and retire from the world, in order to devote ourselves to acts of worship. The life must be like The Messiah's life—between the mountain and the multitude. He who does nothing but pray will soon cease to pray, or his prayers will become a formal routine. When men take themselves out of social life, away from the sphere of the Believers' duty and burden bearing; when they cease to work earnestly for the Master, who worked earnestly for them, they lose the subject matter of prayer, and have no incentive to devotion. Their prayers become personal and selfish. They cannot pray in regard to the wants of humanity or the upbuilding of The Messiah's kingdom, pleading for strength wherewith to work.

We sustain a loss when we neglect the privilege of associating together to strengthen and encourage one another in the service of God. The truths of His Word lose their vividness and importance in our minds. Our hearts cease to be enlightened and aroused by their sanctifying influence, and we decline in spirituality. In our association as Believers we lose much by lack of sympathy with one another. He who shuts himself up to himself is not filling the position that God designed he should. The proper cultivation of the social elements in our nature brings us into sympathy with others, and is a means of development and strength to us in the service of God.

If Believers would associate together, speaking to each other of the love of God, and of the precious truths of redemption, their own hearts would be refreshed, and they would refresh one another. We may be daily learning more of our heavenly Father, gaining a fresh experience of His grace; then we shall desire to speak of His love; and as we do this, our own hearts will be warmed and encouraged. If we thought and talked more of The Redeemer, and less of self, we should have far more of His presence.

If we would but think of God as often as we have evidence of His care for us, we should keep Him ever in our thoughts, and should delight to talk of Him and to praise Him. We talk of temporal things because we have an interest in them. We talk of our friends because we love them; our joys and our sorrows are bound up with them. Yet we have infinitely greater reason to love God than to love our earthly friends; it should be the most natural thing in the world to make Him first in all our thoughts, to talk of His goodness and tell of His power. The rich gifts He has bestowed upon us were not intended to absorb our thoughts and love so much that we should have nothing to give to God; they are constantly to remind us of Him, and to bind us in bonds of love and gratitude to our heavenly Benefactor. We dwell too near the lowlands of earth. Let us raise our eyes to the open door of the sanctuary above, where the light of the glory of God shines in the face of The Messiah, who is able also to save them to the uttermost that come unto God by Him.

We need to praise God more "for His goodness, and for His wonderful works to the children of men." Psalm 107:8. Our devotional exercises should not consist wholly in asking and receiving. Let us not be always thinking of our wants, and never of the benefits we receive. We do not pray any too much, but we are too sparing of giving thanks. We are the constant recipients of God's mercies, and yet how little gratitude we express, how little we praise Him for what He has done for us.

Anciently the Lord bade Israel, when they met together for His service, "Ye shall eat before the Lord your God, and ye shall rejoice in all that ye put your hand unto, ye and your households, wherein the Lord thy God hath blessed thee." Deuteronomy 12:7. That which is done for the glory of God should be done with cheerfulness, with songs of praise and thanksgiving, not with sadness and gloom.

Our God is a tender, merciful Father. His service should not be looked upon as a heart-saddening, distressing exercise. It should be a pleasure to worship the Lord and to take part in His work. God would not have His children, for whom so great salvation has been provided, act as if He were a hard, exacting taskmaster. He is their best friend; and when they worship Him, He expects to be with them, to bless and comfort them, filling their hearts with joy and love. The Lord desires His children to take comfort in His service, and to find more pleasure than hardship in His work. He desires that those who come to worship Him shall carry away with them precious thoughts of His care and love, that they may be cheered in all the employments of daily life, that they may have grace to deal honestly and faithfully in all things.

The Messiah—high and lifted up should be the theme of contemplation, of conversation, and of our most joyful emotion. We should keep in our thoughts every blessing we receive from God, and when we realize His great love, we should be willing to trust everything to the hands of The Messiah who died for our sins.

The soul may ascend nearer heaven on the wings of praise. God is worshiped with song and music in the courts above, and as we express our gratitude, we are approximating to the worship of the heavenly hosts. "Whoso offereth praise glorifieth" God. Psalm 50:23. Let us with reverent joy come before our Creator, with "thanksgiving, and the voice of melody." Isaiah 51:3.

CHAPTER 12

Overcoming Doubt

MANY, ESPECIALLY THOSE who are young Believers in The Messiah, are at times troubled with the suggestions of skepticism. There are in the Bible many things which they cannot explain, or even understand, and Satan employs these to shake their faith in the Scriptures as a revelation from God. They ask, "How shall I know the right way? If the Bible is indeed the Word of God, how can I be freed from these doubts and perplexities?"

God never asks us to believe, without giving sufficient evidence upon which to base our faith. His existence, His character, the truthfulness of His Word, are all established by testimony that appeals to our reason; and this testimony is abundant. Yet God has never removed the possibility of doubt. Our faith must rest upon evidence, not demonstration. Those who wish to doubt will have opportunity; while those who really desire to know the truth, will find plenty of evidence on which to rest their faith.

It is impossible for finite minds fully to comprehend the character or the works of the Infinite One. To the keenest intellect, the most highly educated mind, that holy Being must ever remain clothed in mystery. "Canst thou by searching find out God? canst thou find out the Almighty unto perfection? It is as high as heaven; what canst thou do? deeper than hell; what canst thou know?" Job 11:7, 8.

O the depth of the riches both of the wisdom and knowledge of God! how unsearchable are His judgments, and His ways past finding out! But though "clouds and darkness are round about Him," "righteousness and judgment are the foundation of His throne." Psalm 97:2. We can so far comprehend His dealings with us, and the motives by which He is actuated, that we may discern boundless love and mercy united to infinite power. We can understand as much of His purposes as it is for our good to know; and beyond this we must still trust the hand that is omnipotent, the heart that is full of love.

The Word of God, like the character of its divine Author, presents mysteries that can never be fully comprehended by finite beings. The entrance of sin into the world, the incarnation of The Messiah, regeneration, the resurrection, and many other subjects presented in the Bible, are mysteries too deep for the human mind to explain, or even fully to comprehend. But we have no reason to doubt God's Word because we cannot understand the mysteries of His providence. In the natural world we are constantly surrounded with mysteries that we cannot fathom. The very humblest forms of life present a problem that the wisest of philosophers is powerless to explain. Everywhere are wonders beyond our ken. Should we then be surprised to find that in the spiritual world also there are mysteries that we cannot fathom? The difficulty lies solely in the weakness and narrowness of the human mind. God has given us in the Scriptures sufficient evidence of their divine character, and we are not to doubt His Word because we cannot understand all the mysteries of His providence. There are in Scripture things hard to be understood, which they that are unlearned and unstable wrest unto their own destruction. The difficulties of Scripture have been urged by skeptics as an argument against the Bible; but so far from this, they constitute a strong evidence of its divine inspiration. If it contained no account of God but that which we could easily comprehend; if His greatness and majesty could be grasped by finite minds, then the Bible would not bear the unmistakable credentials of divine authority. The very grandeur and mystery of the themes presented, should inspire faith in it as the Word of God.

The Bible unfolds truth with a simplicity and a perfect adaptation to the needs and longings of the human heart, that has astonished and charmed the most highly cultivated minds, while it enables the humblest and uncultured to discern the way of salvation. And yet these simply stated truths lay hold upon subjects so elevated, so far-reaching, so infinitely beyond the power of human comprehension, that we can accept them only because God has declared them. Thus the plan of redemption is laid open to us, so that every soul may see the steps he is to take in repentance toward God, and faith toward our Lord The Redeemer Messiah, in order to be saved in God's appointed way; yet beneath these truths, so easily understood, lie mysteries that are the hiding of His glory—mysteries that overpower the mind in its research, yet inspire the sincere seeker for truth with reverence and faith. The more he searches the Bible, the deeper is his conviction that it is the word of the living God, and human reason bows before the majesty of divine revelation.

To acknowledge that we cannot fully comprehend the great truths of the Bible is only to admit that the finite mind is inadequate to grasp the infinite; that man, with his limited, human knowledge, cannot understand the purposes of Omniscience.

Because they cannot fathom all its mysteries, the skeptic and the infidel reject God's Word; and not all who profess to believe the Bible are free from danger on this point. Take care friend lest there be in any of you an evil heart of unbelief, in departing from the living God. It is right to study closely the teachings of the Bible, and to search into the deep things of God, so far as they are revealed in Scripture. "While the secret things belong unto the Lord our God", "those things which are revealed belong to us". Deuteronomy 29:29. But it is Satan's work to pervert the investigative powers of the mind. A certain pride is mingled with the consideration of Bible truth, so that men feel impatient and defeated if they cannot explain every portion of Scripture to their satisfaction. It is too humiliating to them to acknowledge that they do not understand the inspired words. They are unwilling to wait patiently until God shall see fit to reveal the truth to them. They feel that their unaided human wisdom is sufficient to enable them to comprehend the Scripture, and failing to do this, they virtually deny its authority. It is true that many theories and doctrines popularly supposed to be derived from the Bible have no foundation in its teaching, and indeed are contrary to the whole tenor of inspiration. These things have been a cause of doubt and perplexity to many minds. They are not, however, chargeable to God's Word, but to man's perversion of it.

If it were possible for created beings to attain to a full understanding of God and His works, then, having reached this point, there would be for them no further discovery of truth, no growth in knowledge, no further development of mind or heart. God would no longer be supreme; and man, having reached the limit of knowledge and attainment, would cease to advance. Let us thank God that it is not so. God is infinite; in Him are all the treasures of wisdom and knowledge. And to all eternity men may be ever searching, ever learning, and yet never exhaust the treasures of His wisdom, His goodness, and His power.

God intends that even in this life the truths of His Word shall be ever unfolding to His people. There is only one way in which this knowledge can be obtained. We can attain to an understanding of God's Word only through the illumination of that Spirit by which the Word was given. The Saviour's promise to His followers was, when He, the Spirit of truth, is come, He will guide you into all truth. For He shall receive of Mine, and shall show it unto you.

God desires man to exercise his reasoning powers; and the study of the Bible will strengthen and elevate the mind as no other study can. Yet we are to beware of deifying reason, which is subject to the weakness and infirmity of humanity. If we would not have the Scriptures clouded to our understanding, so that the plainest truths shall not be comprehended, we must have the simplicity and faith of a little child, ready to learn, and beseeching the aid of the Holy Spirit. A sense of the power and wisdom of God, and of our inability to comprehend His greatness, should inspire us with humility, and we should open His Word, as we would enter His presence, with holy awe. When we come to the Bible, reason must acknowledge an authority superior to itself, and heart and intellect must bow to the great I AM.

There are many things apparently difficult or obscure, which God will make plain and simple to those who thus seek an understanding of them. But without the guidance of the Holy Spirit we shall be continually liable to wrest the Scriptures or to misinterpret them. There is much reading of the Bible that is without profit, and in many cases a positive injury. When the Word of God is opened without reverence and without prayer; when the thoughts and affections are not fixed upon God, or in harmony with His will, the mind is clouded with doubt; and in the very study of the Bible, skepticism strengthens. The enemy takes control of the thoughts, and he suggests interpretations that are not correct. Whenever men are not in word and deed seeking to be in harmony with God, then, however learned they may be, they are liable to err in their understanding of Scripture, and it is not safe to trust to their explanations. Those who look to the Scriptures to find discrepancies, have not spiritual insight.

With distorted vision they will see many causes for doubt and unbelief in things that are really plain and simple.

Disguise it as they may, the real cause of doubt and skepticism, in most cases, is the love of sin. The teachings and restrictions of God's Word are not welcome to the proud, sin-loving heart, and those who are unwilling to obey its requirements are ready to doubt its authority. In order to arrive at truth, we must have a sincere desire to know the truth, and a willingness of heart to obey it. And all who come in this spirit to the study of the Bible, will find abundant evidence that it is God's Word, and they may gain an understanding of its truths that will make them wise unto salvation.

The Messiah has said, If any man will to do His will, he shall know whether it be of God. Instead of questioning and caviling concerning that which you do not understand, give heed to the light that already shines upon you, and you will receive greater light. By the grace of The Messiah, perform every duty that has been made plain to your understanding, and you will be enabled to understand and perform those of which you are now in doubt.

There is an evidence that is open to all—the most highly educated, and the most illiterate—the evidence of experience. God invites us to prove for ourselves the reality of His Word, the truth of His promises. He bids us "taste and see that the Lord is good." Psalm 34:8. Instead of depending upon the word of another, we are to taste for ourselves. He declares, ask, and ye shall receive. His promises will be fulfilled. They have never failed; they never can fail. And as we draw near to The Redeemer, and rejoice in the fullness of His love, our doubt and darkness will disappear in the light of His presence.

God hath delivered us from the power of darkness, and hath translated us into the kingdom of His dear Son. And every one who has passed from death unto life is able to set to his seal that God is true. He can testify, I needed help, and I found it in The Redeemer. Every want was supplied, the hunger of my soul was satisfied; and now the Bible is to me the revelation of The Redeemer—Messiah. Do you ask why I believe in the Redeemer?—Because He is to me a divine Saviour. Why do I believe the Bible?—Because I have found it to be the voice of God to my soul. We may have the witness in ourselves that the Bible is true, that The Messiah is the Son of God. We know that we are not following cunningly devised fables.

When the people of God are growing in grace, they will be constantly obtaining a clearer understanding of His Word. They will discern new light and beauty in its sacred truths. This has been true in the history of the house of God in all ages, and thus it will continue to the end. "The path of the righteous is as the light of dawn, that shineth more and more unto the perfect day." Proverbs 4:18.

By faith we may look to the hereafter, and grasp the pledge of God for a growth of intellect, the human faculties uniting with the divine, and every power of the soul being brought into direct contact with the Source of light. We may rejoice that all which has perplexed us in the providences of God will then be made plain, things hard to be understood will then find an explanation; and where our finite minds discovered only confusion and broken purposes, we shall see the most perfect and beautiful harmony. Now we see through a glass, darkly; but then face to face: now I know in part; but then shall I know even as also I am known.

CHAPTER 13

Rejoicing Within

THE CHILDREN OF GOD are called to be representatives of The Messiah, showing forth the goodness and mercy of the Lord. As The Redeemer has revealed to us the true character of the Father, so we are to reveal The Messiah to a world that does not know His tender, pitying love. In every one of His children, The Redeemer sends a letter to the world. If you are The Messiah's follower, He sends in you a letter to the family, the village, the street, where you live. The Redeemer, dwelling in you, desires to speak to the hearts of those who are not acquainted with Him. Perhaps they do not read the Bible, or do not hear the voice that speaks to them in its pages; they do not see the love of God through His works. But if you are a true representative of The Redeemer, it may be that through you they will be led to understand something of His goodness, and be won to love and serve Him.

Believers are set as light bearers on the way to heaven. They are to reflect to the world the light shining upon them from The Messiah. Their life and character should be such that through them others will get a right conception of The Messiah and of His service.

If we do represent The Messiah, we shall make His service appear attractive, as it really is. Believers who gather up gloom and sadness to their souls, and murmur and complain, are giving to others a false representation of God and the Believers life. They give the impression that God is not pleased to have His children happy, and in this they bear false witness against our heavenly Father.

Satan is exultant when he can lead the children of God into unbelief and despondency. He delights to see us mistrusting God, doubting His willingness and power to save us. He loves to have us feel that the Lord will do us harm by His providences. It is the work of Satan to represent the Lord as lacking in compassion and pity. He misstates the truth in regard to Him. He fills the imagination with false ideas concerning God; and instead of dwelling upon the truth in regard to our heavenly Father, we too often fix our minds upon the misrepresentations of Satan, and dishonor God by

distrusting Him and murmuring against Him. Satan ever seeks
to make the religious life one of gloom. He desires it to appear
toilsome and difficult; and when the Believer presents in his
own life this view of religion, he is, through his unbelief,
seconding the falsehood of Satan.

Many, walking along the path of life, dwell upon their
mistakes and failures and disappointments, and their hearts are
filled with grief and discouragement. While I was in Europe, a
sister who had been doing this, and who was in deep distress,
wrote to me, asking for some word of encouragement. The
night after I had read her letter, I dreamed that I was in a
garden, and one who seemed to be the owner of the garden was
conducting me through its paths. I was gathering the flowers
and enjoying their fragrance, when this sister, who had been
walking by my side, called my attention to some unsightly
briers that were impeding her way. There she was mourning
and grieving. She was not walking in the pathway, following
the guide, but was walking among the briers and thorns. "Oh,"
she mourned, "is it not a pity that this beautiful garden is
spoiled with thorns?" Then the guide said, "Let the thorns
alone, for they will only wound you. Gather the roses, the
lilies, and the pin
ks."

Have there not been some bright spots in your experience?
Have you not had some precious seasons when your heart
throbbed with joy in response to the Spirit of God? When you
look back into the chapters of your life experience, do you not
find some pleasant pages? Are not God's promises, like the
fragrant flowers, growing beside your path on every hand?
Will you not let their beauty and sweetness fill your heart with
joy?

The briers and thorns will only wound and grieve you; and
if you gather only these things, and present them to others, are
you not, besides slighting the goodness of God yourself,
preventing those around you from walking in the path of life?

It is not wise to gather together all the unpleasant
recollections of a past life—its iniquities and
disappointments—to talk over them and mourn over them until
we are overwhelmed with discouragement. A discouraged soul
is filled with darkness, shutting out the light of God from his
own soul, and casting a shadow upon the pathway of others.

Thank God for the bright pictures which He has presented
to us. Let us group together the blessed assurances of His love,

that we may look upon them continually: The Son of God leaving His Father's throne, clothing His divinity with humanity, that He might rescue man from the power of Satan; His triumph in our behalf, opening heaven to men, revealing to human vision the presence chamber where the Deity unveils His glory; the fallen race uplifted from the pit of ruin into which sin had plunged it, and brought again into connection with the infinite God, and having endured the divine test through faith in our Redeemer, clothed in the righteousness of The Messiah, and exalted to His throne—these are the pictures which God would have us contemplate.

When we seem to doubt God's love, and distrust His promises, we dishonor Him and grieve His Holy Spirit. How would a mother feel if her children were constantly complaining of her, just as though she did not mean them well, when her whole life's effort had been to forward their interests and to give them comfort? Suppose they should doubt her love; it would break her heart. How would any parent feel to be thus treated by his children? And how can our heavenly Father regard us when we distrust His love, which has led Him to give His only begotten Son that we might have life? He that spared not His own Son, but delivered Him up for us all, how shall He not with Him also freely give us all things? And yet how many, by their actions, if not in word, are saying, The Lord does not mean this for me. Perhaps He loves others, but He does not love me.

All this is harming your own soul; for every word of doubt you utter is inviting Satan's temptations; it is strengthening in you the tendency to doubt, and it is grieving from you the ministering angels. When Satan tempts you, breathe not a word of doubt or darkness. If you choose to open the door to his suggestions, your mind will be filled with distrust and rebellious questioning. If you talk out your feelings, every doubt you express not only reacts upon yourself, but it is a seed that will germinate and bear fruit in the life of others, and it may be impossible to counteract the influence of your words. You yourself may be able to recover from the season of temptation and from the snare of Satan, but others, who have been swayed by your influence, may not be able to escape from the unbelief you have suggested. How important that we speak only those things that will give spiritual strength and life!

Angels are listening to hear what kind of report you are bearing to the world about your heavenly Master. Let your conversation be of Him who liveth to make intercession for you before the Father. When you take the hand of a friend, let praise to God be on your lips and in your heart. This will attract his thoughts to The Redeemer.

All have trials; griefs hard to bear, temptations hard to resist. Do not tell your troubles to your fellow mortals, but carry everything to God in prayer. Make it a rule never to utter one word of doubt or discouragement. You can do much to brighten the life of others and strengthen their efforts, by words of hope and holy cheer.

There is many a brave soul sorely pressed by temptation, almost ready to faint in the conflict with self and with the powers of evil. Do not discourage such a one in his hard struggle. Cheer him with brave, hopeful words that shall urge him on his way. Thus the light of The Messiah may shine from you. None of us lives to himself. By our unconscious influence others may be encouraged and strengthened, or they may be discouraged, and repelled from The Messiah and the truth.

There are many who have an erroneous idea of the life and character of The Messiah. They think that He was devoid of warmth and sunniness, that He was stern, severe, and joyless. In many cases the whole religious experience is colored by these gloomy views.

It is often said that The Redeemer wept, but that He was never known to smile. Our Saviour was indeed a Man of Sorrows, and acquainted with grief, for He opened His heart to all the woes of men. But though His life was self-denying and shadowed with pain and care, His spirit was not crushed. His countenance did not wear an expression of grief and repining, but ever one of peaceful serenity. His heart was a wellspring of life; and wherever He went, He carried rest and peace, joy and gladness.

Our Saviour was deeply serious and intensely in earnest, but never gloomy or morose. The life of those who imitate Him will be full of earnest purpose; they will have a deep sense of personal responsibility. Levity will be repressed; there will be no boisterous merriment, no rude jesting; but the religion of The Redeemer gives peace like a river. It does not quench the light of joy; it does not restrain cheerfulness, nor cloud the sunny, smiling face. The Messiah came not to be ministered unto but to minister; and when His love reigns in the heart, we shall follow His example.

If we keep uppermost in our minds the unkind and unjust acts of others, we shall find it impossible to love them as The Messiah has loved us; but if our thoughts dwell upon the wondrous love and pity of The Messiah for us, the same spirit will flow out to others. We should love and respect one another, notwithstanding the faults and imperfections that we cannot help seeing. Humility and self-distrust should be cultivated, and a patient tenderness with the faults of others. This will kill out all narrowing selfishness, and make us largehearted and generous.

The psalmist says, "Trust in the Lord, and do good; so shalt thou dwell in the land, and verily, thou shalt be fed." Psalm 37:3. "Trust in the Lord." Each day has its burdens, its cares and perplexities; and when we meet, how ready we are to talk of our difficulties and trials. So many borrowed troubles intrude, so many fears are indulged, such a weight of anxiety is expressed, that one might suppose we had no pitying, loving Saviour, ready to hear all our requests, and to be to us a present help in every time of need.

Some are always fearing, and borrowing trouble. Every day they are surrounded with the tokens of God's love; every day they are enjoying the bounties of His providence; but they overlook these present blessings. Their minds are continually dwelling upon something disagreeable, which they fear may come; or some difficulty may really exist, which, though small, blinds their eyes to the many things that demand gratitude. The difficulties they encounter, instead of driving them to God, the only source of their help, separate them from Him, because they awaken unrest and repining.

Do we well to be thus unbelieving? Why should we be ungrateful and distrustful? The Redeemer is our friend; all heaven is interested in our welfare. We should not allow the perplexities and worries of everyday life to fret the mind and cloud the brow. If we do, we shall always have something to vex and annoy. We should not indulge a solicitude that only frets and wears us, but does not help us to bear trials.

You may be perplexed in business; your prospects may grow darker and darker, and you may be threatened with loss; but do not become discouraged; cast your care upon God, and remain calm and cheerful. Pray for wisdom to manage your affairs with discretion, and thus prevent loss and disaster. Do all you can on your part to bring about favorable results. The Redeemer has promised His aid, but not apart from our effort.

When, relying upon our Helper, you have done all you can, accept the result cheerfully.

It is not the will of God that His people should be weighed down with care. But our Lord does not deceive us. He does not say to us, Do not fear; there are no dangers in your path. He knows there are trials and dangers, and He deals with us plainly. He does not propose to take His people out of a world of sin and evil, but He points them to a never-failing refuge.

In His Sermon on the Mount, The Messiah taught His disciples precious lessons in regard to the necessity of trusting in God. These lessons were designed to encourage the children of God through all ages, and they have come down to our time full of instruction and comfort. The Saviour pointed His followers to the birds of the air as they warbled their carols of praise, unencumbered with thoughts of care, for they sow not, neither do they reap. And yet the great Father provides for their needs. Are you not much better than they? The great Provider for man and beast opens His hand and supplies all His creatures. The birds of the air are not beneath His notice. He does not drop the food into their bills, but He makes provision for their needs. They must gather the grains He has scattered for them. They must prepare the material for their little nests. They must feed their young. They go forth singing to their labor, for your heavenly Father feedeth them. And are ye not much better than they? Are not you, as intelligent, spiritual worshipers, of more value than the birds of the air? Will not the Author of our being, the Preserver of our life, the One who formed us in His own divine image, provide for our necessities if we but trust in Him?

The Messiah pointed His disciples to the flowers of the field, growing in rich profusion, and glowing in the simple beauty which the heavenly Father had given them, as an expression of His love to man. He said, Consider the lilies of the field, how they grow. The beauty and simplicity of these natural flowers far outrival the splendor of Solomon. The most gorgeous attire produced by the skill of art cannot bear comparison with the natural grace and radiant beauty of the flowers of God's creation. The Redeemer says, If God so clothe the grass of the field, which today is, and tomorrow is cast into the oven, shall He not much more clothe you, O ye of little faith? If God, the divine Artist, gives to the simple flowers that perish in a day their delicate and varied colors, how much greater care will He have for those who are created in His own image? This lesson of The Messiah's is a rebuke to the anxious thought, the perplexity and doubt, of the faithless heart.

The Lord would have all His sons and daughters happy, peaceful, and obedient. Happiness that is sought from selfish motives, outside of the path of duty, is ill-balanced, fitful, and transitory; it passes away, and the soul is filled with loneliness and sorrow; but there is joy and satisfaction in the service of God; the Believer is not left to walk in uncertain paths; he is not left to vain regrets and disappointments. If we do not have the pleasures of this life, we may still be joyful in looking to the life beyond.

But even here Believers may have the joy of communion with The Messiah; they may have the light of His love, the perpetual comfort of His presence. Every step in life may bring us closer to The Redeemer, may give us a deeper experience of His love, and may bring us one step nearer to the blessed home of peace. Then let us not cast away our confidence, but have firm assurance, firmer than ever before. "Hitherto hath the Lord helped us" 1 Samuel 7:12, and He will help us to the end. Let us look to the monumental pillars, reminders of what the Lord has done to comfort us and to save us from the hand of the destroyer. Let us keep fresh in our memory all the tender mercies that God has shown us—the tears He has wiped away, the pains He has soothed, the anxieties removed, the fears dispelled, the wants supplied, the blessings bestowed—thus strengthening ourselves for all that is before us through the remainder of our pilgrimage.

We cannot but look forward to new perplexities in the coming conflict, but we may look on what is past as well as on what is to come, and say, "Hitherto hath the Lord helped us." "As thy days, so shall thy strength be." Deuteronomy 33:25. The trial will not exceed the strength that shall be given us to bear it. Then let us take up our work just where we find it, believing that whatever may come, strength proportionate to the trial will be given.

And by and by the gates of heaven will be thrown open to admit God's children, and from the lips of the King of glory the benediction will fall on their ears like richest music, Come, ye blessed of My Father, inherit the kingdom prepared for you from the foundation of the world.

Then the redeemed will be welcomed to the home that The Redeemer is preparing for them. There their companions will not be the vile of earth, liars, idolators, the impure, and unbelieving; but they will associate with those who have overcome Satan, and through divine grace have formed perfect characters. Every sinful tendency, every imperfection, that afflicts them here, has been removed by the blood of The Messiah, and the excellence and brightness of His glory, far exceeding the brightness of the sun, is imparted to them. And the moral beauty, the perfection of His character, shines through them, in worth far exceeding this outward splendor. They are without fault before the great white throne, sharing the dignity and the privileges of the angels.In view of the glorious inheritance that may be his, what shall a man give in exchange for his soul? He may be poor, yet he possesses in himself a wealth and dignity that the world could never bestow. The soul redeemed and cleansed from sin, with all its noble powers dedicated to the service of God, is of surpassing worth; and there is joy in heaven in the presence of God and the holy angels over one soul redeemed, a joy that is expressed in songs of holy triumph.

srh

Notes

NOTES

NOTES

NOTES

NOTES

NOTES

NOTES

NOTES